Angela Hartnett's Cucina

One of the brightest talents to have emerged on the UK food scene in the past few years, Angela Hartnett has been described by Gordon Ramsay as 'the new Elizabeth David'. As one of the few female British chefs to hold a Michelin star, her innovative cooking has been commended by reviewers and fellow chefs alike.

But Angela's real inspiration comes from the food she grew up with – the classic dishes that she learned at her Italian grandmother's side. This is a unique collection of the family recipes that Angela has nurtured and developed over the years, and a celebration of the fantastic tastes, aromas and textures of Italian cooking that she loved from childhood.

With stunning food photography by Jonathan Lovekin, and 140 evocative and accessible recipes, *Angela Hartnett's Cucina* brings the warmth of the Italian family kitchen to your home.

About the Author

Angela Hartnett became chef-patron at London's Connaught Hotel in October 2002 after training at Gordon Ramsay's restaurants Aubergine, Petrus and Amaryllis, followed by a stint at Verre in Dubai. She appeared alongside Gordon on ITV's *Hell's Kitchen* in 2004. Angela has rapidly established herself as one of the most high-profile women in international catering. Her individual style of cooking is achieved 'through combining great Mediterranean cuisine with a modern European influence'. Angela's restaurant MENU at the Connaught was awarded a Michelin star in 2004. She opened her first US restaurant in Miami in 2007 and her first television series for the BBC will be broadcast later the same year. Angela was awarded an MBE in the 2007 New Year's Honour's List for services to the hospitality industry.

ANGELA HARTNETT'S CUCINA

THREE GENERATIONS OF ITALIAN FAMILY COOKING

EBURY
PRESS

1 3 5 7 9 10 8 6 4 2

Published in 2007 by Ebury Press, an imprint
of Ebury Publishing

Ebury Publishing is a division of the Random
House Group

The Random House Group Limited Reg. No. 954009

Addresses for companies within the Random House
Group can be found at www.randomhouse.co.uk

A CIP catalogue record for this book is available
from the British Library

The Random House Group Limited makes every
effort to ensure that the papers used in our books are
made from trees that have been legally sourced from
well-managed and credibly certified forests.
Our paper procurement policy can be found on
www.randomhouse.co.uk

Food and cover photography: Jonathan Lovekin
Art direction and design: BLOK
Copy editor: Patricia Burgess
Illustrator: Monika Aichele

Printed and bound in Italy by Graphicom

ISBN 9780091910273

Previous page: Great Uncle Dorino and Auntie Viv
outside Bosco, the family house in Bardi, Italy, *c.* 1948

General notes

All olive oil is extra virgin unless specified otherwise – don't accept anything less.

All butter is unsalted unless specified otherwise.

All sugar is caster sugar unless specified otherwise.

All eggs are large and organic or free-range unless specified otherwise.

All fresh herbs, fruit and vegetables should be washed before use.

All milk is full-fat unless specified otherwise.

All onions and garlic should be peeled unless specified otherwise.

All lemons should be unwaxed.

I prefer Maldon sea salt but occasionally a recipe may refer to rock salt.

Foreword by Gordon Ramsay, OBE

Angela Hartnett is one of the most exciting cooks we have in the UK today, and I am hugely proud to have played a part in her career. From the first shift that she worked at Aubergine, it was clear that she was something special. She is one of the small number of chefs with a university degree, and the fact that she chose cooking over other, more comfortable career options is indicative of the passion and commitment she has always shown, qualities that have helped her rise to the top of her profession and become a role model for so many aspiring women in the catering industry.

Angela is a natural cook, in the sense that it is in her blood. She comes from a big, boisterous Italian family, where cooking and eating were at the very heart of life. She grew up with a great appreciation of honest, simple cooking, where the flavour and integrity of the ingredients come first. This foundation formed the perfect platform for her to master the technical demands of a Michelin-starred kitchen. It is the convergence of her Italian roots and her classical training that forms her unique style of cooking, or 'cucina'. The perfect example of this is crostata (see page 194) – I'm always impressed that she serves such a rustic, Italian family dish as part of afternoon tea at a very English hotel!

Angela has no airs and graces and is warm and natural with everybody she meets: from the most junior member of her brigade to the most feared and revered restaurant critic, she is always just Ange. Her personality shines through in these recipes, making this book as warm and engaging as Angela herself. This is a book for everybody who shares Angela's joy for food.

Dedicated to my Nonna and all my family

I always find it fascinating how football matches and other sporting events bring out people's true allegiances. In my case, my heart lies with Italy first and foremost. Even though I was born in the UK and have lived here most of my life, I constantly find myself drawn towards that big boot shape in the Mediterranean.

My maternal grandparents were from a small village called Bardi, in the Emilia-Romagna region of Italy, but they moved to Wales in the 1930s. My mother was born in the Rhonda valley and grew up speaking Italian at home and English at school. When she was in her late teens, the whole family moved from Wales to Essex, and my grandfather and his two brothers (who had also come over from Italy) each opened a fish and chip shop – in Becontree, Barking and Dagenham Heathway. It might not have been the most obvious trade for immigrants from an inland region of Italy, but business was good and the families prospered.

I was born in Canterbury in Kent, and grew up in Densole, near Folkestone. Sadly, my father died when I was just seven, and my mother was left with three children under the age of ten. Mum decided to move back to Essex to be nearer to both sets of grandparents, and we lived over the fish and chip shop in Becontree for the first six months while we looked for a permanent home. Eventually, we found a place in Upminster, only 15 minutes' away from Nonna's (my Italian grandmother), and this is really where my culinary education began.

My first real cooking job was helping in the fish and chip shop. When I was fifteen I spent every Friday night working there. I would finish work around eight o'clock, take the Tube back to Upminster, jump in the shower and be at a nightclub with my friends by ten o'clock.

Grandmothers and granddaughters

In Italian families, it's always the job of the women in the house to keep things running, and as the eldest granddaughter, it was officially my duty to step in if Nonna needed any help with shopping, cleaning or cooking. Mum was usually at work or looking after my siblings, Michael and Anne, so I spent most of my teenage years helping my grandmother to cook the family meals. Nonna would solemnly summon me to the house to help her make tortelli and ravioli, or send me out to the shops to buy ingredients. Both she and my mother taught me an appreciation of fresh produce and the importance of always buying the best you can possibly afford. I remember once bringing home fruit and vegetables that Nonna judged substandard – she sent me back to the shop to complain! I was too shy to make a fuss, so I went back and paid for new produce with my own pocket money.

Above
Great Auntie Ilda with
my grandfather in his very
first fish and chip shop in
Ferndale, in Wales's
Rhondda Valley

Previous page
My mum in 1937 with her
parents, Nonna and my
grandfather

Above
The first rule of cooking:
taste everything yourself
as you make it

Right
Me (aged 5) and my
brother Michael (aged 7)

Overleaf
Me in the kitchens at the
Connaught, 2005

Those years of shopping and cooking for Nonna taught me to understand what great Italian cooking is all about: start with the very best raw ingredients and do very little to them; just let them speak for themselves, and make the best of their natural flavours and textures. I really felt that I proved my cooking abilities to my grandmother during this time; I certainly made better desserts than her, but (as she told me by way of excuse) Italians don't really go in for desserts.

Leaving home

When I left home and went to study history at college in Cambridge, I still loved making Italian dishes – chicken cacciatore, ragùs, risottos. I lived in a shared house and I would arrive at the beginning of each term with boxes of dried mushrooms, pasta and Parmesan. Every so often Nonna would summon me home to help make celebratory anolini (page 76), and together we had a good production line going. Nonna really taught me how to be organized in the kitchen; the rule was 'a place for everything and everything in its place'. She once said to me of my mum (Giuliana) and her sisters: 'Maria's very organized, Viv was organized until she got married, and Giuliana – I don't know where she came from!' These pasta-making sessions at home were a wonderful bonding experience – three generations of women working together, talking and sharing stories.

Even though I loved studying, I always felt I wanted to cook. What drove me was the idea of running my own business and being my own boss, which probably stemmed from seeing how my own family ran the fish and chip shops. After graduating, I worked in Cambridge for two years in various pub and restaurant kitchens, eventually securing a job at the Midsummer House restaurant run by Hans Schweitzer. He took me on as a waitress, but I managed to convince him that I was a good cook, so he gave me my first proper cooking job. In fact, he bought me my first chef's jacket, plus a back-to-basics cookery book to teach me all the things I hadn't learnt so far. After two years, Hans sent me to Barbados, where I spent six months cooking in a restaurant in Tamarind Cove – probably one of the best jobs in my life. We lazed on the beach during the day, worked in the restaurant only in the evenings, and by ten o'clock we were dancing in a club! As great as it was, I was conscious that this wasn't going to help my career very much.

What I'd been waiting for

In the summer of 1994 I started doing trial days in various London restaurants. At that time London was just starting to become a major culinary centre, and one of the new kids on the block was a certain Gordon Ramsay. I read a newspaper article that named him as the most exciting person working on the London restaurant scene, and knew instantly that Gordon's was the place I wanted to work. I wrote to him and he let me work in the kitchen for one day – starting at 8 a.m. and finishing 17 hours later at 1 a.m. As tiring, frantic and stressful as it undoubtedly was, the experience was above all inspirational and enthralling. Gordon was so energetic and passionate – it made me want to be a permanent part of that team. And what a team it was: Marcus Wareing, Mark Askew and I are all chefs in our own right these days, and I have to thank Gordon here and now for giving me my first proper opportunity. Although I had very little experience and no traditional training, he took me on in good faith and furthered my education as a chef.

Life wasn't easy, though. I remember once arriving slightly late at the Aubergine restaurant (probably about 7.20 a.m. as opposed to the normal 7 a.m.), then immediately managing to split a vanilla anglaise, overcook some crèmes brûlées, and cover the whole kitchen in sweet pastry. Then, in the process of cleaning up the pastry, I accidentally switched off the fridge so that all the sorbets melted before lunch. Despite hiccups like these, Gordon was ever the gentleman and would always let me leave early. One night he was insisting to the guys that they let me go home early, but I sat him down and explained that I didn't want any special treatment. He never insisted again, and I have to say that I lived to regret my request – it was exhausting!

During my last year at Aubergine, 1995, Nonna became very ill. I visited her every Sunday and, when possible, we would have family meals at the restaurant. Sadly, Nonna died before she could see me go on to become a successful head chef. I hope she knows how much I owe to her.

I spent the next nine years working in various restaurants under Gordon's direction – London, Scotland, back to London – and then I set up his first venture abroad, in Dubai. When I returned to the UK it was to the prospect of running my very own restaurant – this would mean I'd really made it. But the Connaught Hotel and Dining Room was not quite what I'd imagined, and my appointment caused uproar. The Connaught was a place of tradition and the food hadn't changed in years (if ever). For a woman to come in and turn the place on its head was a huge shock for residents and staff. Initially, we kept the old Grill Room classics on the menu and just ran my Italian-influenced menu in the main dining room. I don't deny it was tough, and I had to face a lot of opposition, but it was all worth it. We were awarded a Michelin star within the first year of opening, and I established my cuisine as predominant over the old-school favourites.

Full circle

For my family, food has always been an important part of our gatherings. Whenever anyone's back from Italy or simply comes to visit (which is pretty often), there's a gathering of the clan. While doing research for this book, I visited Bardi with three girlfriends and we found ourselves on the receiving end of a generous and delicious array of food. One day, after a big lunch, we went first to the home of Auntie Maria, where we were offered a torta and crostata; then, at my cousin Rosanna's, we had another crostata with tea; finally, at cousin Paul and Antonia's, we ate torta di patata and Antonia's delicious cake. My friends quickly found out that you cannot say no to fantastic Italian home cooking. It's always, 'Just a small piece, just have a little taste...' Before you know it, your waistband is struggling to contain your increasing girth.

Four years after opening the restaurant at the Connaught, things came full circle. I held a surprise party for Mum's seventieth birthday in the Connaught's private dining room, and relatives made the journey from all parts of the world. It was wonderful. Memorably, my brother told us all a story that night. Apparently, the day before we opened at the Connaught he'd had a call from Mum. She'd been up all night worrying and felt she had to confide in him. 'Michael, I love my daughter,' she said, 'but do you think she can cook?' I'm happy to say that the party established that I can cook, and Mum's mind is now at rest.

My family have influenced me so much in my career and my cooking, particularly Nonna, and my mum and her sisters and cousins. As a chef you are constantly learning and developing, and the Connaught has allowed me not only to make my cooking more sophisticated, but to expand on those Italian influences, pulling in ideas, experiences and inspiration from all over the world to create my own cuisine. I'm continuing the family tradition in my own way and I feel lucky and proud to have learned so much from them.

Above
Mum and I deep in
conversation, July 2006

Right
My nephew Finn (aged 4)
and I, when he was visiting
from New York in July
2006

Soups

One of my strongest food memories from childhood is of hot, steaming bowls of minestrone. My Nonna, of course, made the best, with Auntie Maria's a strong second (sorry, Mum!). Minestrone got me into terrible trouble with Nonna one summer. I was due to start at a new secondary school, but Mum had sent me over to Italy with my baby cousin, Patrik, which meant I would miss the first week of term. My brother Michael, stirring in the way that siblings often do, told me that I had been sent only because they wanted a babysitter. I was stomping around in a temper and didn't notice that Nonna had left a big pot of minestrone cooling on the balcony. I accidentally sent it flying and Nonna's wrath descended on me like a ton of bricks. I think it's the only time she's been truly angry with me. After sulking shamefacedly in my room for two weeks, I was sent back to England early.

Types of soup vary across Italy. In Tuscany, for instance, soups are an essential part of the regional cuisine; in the Veneto region they serve wet risottos that are more like soups than main courses; and in Emilia-Romagna pulses and beans are key ingredients. Minestrone has always been a family favourite, but since I started cooking professionally I've become more adventurous in my soup-making. The important thing is to use fresh, seasonal ingredients and beautiful seasoning: if you get the combination right, a lovely soup is unbeatable, in my view. At the Connaught we like to serve a small portion of soup as an appetizer – it really gets the tastebuds going. One of the first soups I ever put on the menu was White onion velouté (page 21), which we serve with sautéed frog's legs.

The essence of a good soup or velouté is the same: when you have that first spoonful, what you should taste is the real flavour of the predominant ingredient, whether it's fennel, white onion, pumpkin or whatever. It should be more than just a creamy taste in your mouth. Don't make the mistake of throwing in a bit of everything, otherwise you'll end up with a soup that tastes of nothing in particular.

It's a common misconception that soups need to be cooked for hours. In fact, I think the quicker the cooking time, the more authentic the flavour. A cardinal rule is never to dilute a soup with water; it is far better to use stock. Not only is stock more flavourful, but it's a great way of using up leftover vegetables, meat carcasses and bones.

This chapter will show you that soups are anything but dull. And if, like me, you occasionally fancy something with a bit more 'kick', they can be livened up even further by adding some Salsa verde (page 256), Romesco sauce (page 258) or even a few chopped chillies.

White onion velouté

When people taste this they're always amazed at the intense flavour, which you don't normally expect from onions. It can be served on its own if you like, or jazzed up a little with Salsa verde (page 256).

Serves 4
50 g butter
2 tbsp olive oil
1.5 kg white onions, thinly sliced
1 sprig of fresh thyme
pinch of rock salt
600–800 ml Vegetable stock (page 261)
drizzle of double cream, to serve

Melt the butter in a pan over a low heat and add the olive oil. When hot, add the onions, thyme and rock salt. Cover with a lid or cartouche (a circle of greaseproof paper), as this will allow the onions to cook quickly but without colouring. Cook gently until softened, about 15 minutes.

Remove the covering and add the stock. Bring to the boil and simmer until the onions are cooked through, about 8–10 minutes.

Transfer the mixture to a food processor or blender and blitz to a purée. For an extra-smooth texture, pass through a fine sieve before returning to a pan to reheat. Correct the consistency of the soup (if necessary) by adding a little more stock. Check the seasoning and serve with a drizzle of double cream.

Creamy mushroom soup

This is a very versatile soup that's full of flavour. For a special occasion, you could put some sautéed fresh ceps (see recipe opposite) in the bottom of each bowl and pop a teaspoon of crème fraîche on top.

Serves 4
500 g Portobello or chestnut mushrooms, wiped clean with a damp cloth
50 g butter
1 garlic clove, finely chopped
2 large shallots, finely chopped
200 ml Chicken stock (page 260)
200 ml milk
100 ml double cream
salt and freshly ground black pepper

Cut the stalks off the mushrooms and remove the gills with a teaspoon; discard both. Roughly chop the caps into fairly large pieces.

Heat the butter in a large pan over a low heat. Add the garlic and shallots and cook gently for 3–4 minutes, without colouring, until soft. Add the mushrooms, stir well and cover with a lid. (This allows the mushrooms to steam in the pan and release their water content so that you're left with a concentrated mushroomy taste.) Lower the heat and leave the mushrooms to steam for 3–4 minutes.

Add the chicken stock and milk, then simmer, without the lid, for about 20 minutes.

Allow the mixture to cool a little before blending in a food processor or liquidizer. Pass through a sieve for extra smoothness, if you like. Just before serving, stir in the cream, check the seasoning and reheat gently.

Pumpkin soup

This is a fantastic autumnal soup. Our secret at the Connaught is to put Parmesan rind in the pan when it's cooking, which gives it a lovely depth of flavour. Although I think truffle oil has been overexposed in recent years, a drop of it does finish off this soup very well. You can leave out the sautéed ceps if you prefer.

Serves 4
50 g butter
1 x 1 kg ripe pumpkin or butternut squash, peeled, seeded and cut into 1.5 cm cubes
2 tbsp white wine
rind of Parmesan, about 50 g
1 litre Chicken stock (page 260)
drizzle of double cream (optional)
drizzle of truffle oil (optional)
salt and freshly ground black pepper

To serve (optional)
knob of butter
1 tbsp olive oil
100 g fresh ceps
handful of Parmesan shavings

Heat the 50 g of butter in a large pan until melted. Add the pumpkin and lightly sauté over a low heat, stirring constantly to prevent sticking, for about 10 minutes. It should be soft but not coloured.

Pour in the wine and allow it to bubble and reduce until completely evaporated. Cover with a lid and cook for 8–10 minutes, until the pumpkin is completely tender.

Add the Parmesan rind and all but 200 ml of the chicken stock to the pan and return to the boil. Once boiling, reduce the heat and cook for a further 5 minutes. Remove and discard the Parmesan rind.

Remove the soup from the heat and allow to cool a little before transferring it to a blender or food processor. Whiz until smooth, then pass through a fine sieve. If necessary, correct the consistency with a little more chicken stock or a touch of cream. Check the seasoning.

If you are serving the soup with the sautéed ceps, heat the butter and olive oil in a frying pan over a medium heat. Add the ceps and cook for 2–3 minutes, until golden. Season to taste.

Reheat the soup if necessary, then ladle into individual bowls. Add a drizzle of truffle oil, if liked, the sautéed ceps and a few Parmesan shavings.

Overleaf (left to right)
My cousin Giuliana, Aunt Viviana, Nonna and Uncle Gianni outside the family house in Bardi

Fagioli soup

Beans are a Tuscan ingredient, but they do crop up a lot in Emilia-Romagnan cooking too. This is a really thick, filling broth. If you can't get hold of fresh beans, use good-quality canned ones instead.

Serves 4–6
500 g fresh or 300 g dried borlotti beans
1.75–2.75 litres Vegetable stock
(page 261)
2 celery sticks, chopped into 1 cm cubes
2 carrots, chopped into 1 cm cubes
1 onion, chopped into 1 cm cubes
1 tbsp chopped fresh flatleaf parsley,
to serve
handful of freshly grated Parmesan,
to serve
salt and freshly ground black pepper

If using dried beans, put them in a bowl, cover with water and leave to soak overnight. Drain before using.

Place the fresh or soaked beans in a large pan and cover with cold water. Bring to the boil, then immediately drain and rinse under cold water – this will get rid of any scum that may have risen to the surface.

Place the drained beans in a clean pan and cover with the stock. Add the vegetables and bring to the boil. Reduce the heat and simmer for 1½–2 hours, or until soft.

Check the seasoning and serve with the parsley and Parmesan scattered on top.

Minestrone

This classic Italian soup, which should be thick and served with Parmesan or Pecorino, makes a meal in itself. It does taste better if made with chicken stock, but vegetarians will be glad to know that it's also fine made with vegetable stock. If you want it to be extra-hearty, fry 100 g diced pancetta until brown and crisp and scatter it over the top of the soup with the Parmesan when serving. If you like, you can add a handful of ditalini pasta at the same time as the potato, but you'd have to serve it immediately rather than reheating later, as the pasta will go soggy otherwise.

Serves 4
2 tbsp olive oil
knob of butter
1 sprig of fresh thyme
1 garlic clove, crushed
2 carrots, diced
1 large onion, diced
2 celery sticks, diced
1 head of fennel, diced
about 750 ml Chicken or Vegetable stock
(pages 260–1)
1 potato, diced
1 courgette, diced
2 tbsp finely chopped fresh
flatleaf parsley
handful of freshly grated Parmesan,
to serve
salt and freshly ground black pepper

Heat the olive oil and butter in a heavy-based pan. Add the thyme, garlic and all the vegetables except the courgette and potato. Cook over a medium heat without colouring, stirring constantly, for about 8–10 minutes, until soft.

Add enough stock to cover the vegetables, reduce the heat and simmer for 8–10 minutes.

Add the potato and cook for a further 10 minutes. At this stage the soup can be set aside or refrigerated until ready for use.

When you want to serve the minestrone, reheat it gently and add the diced courgette and parsley. Adjust the seasoning to taste.

Transfer to individual soup bowls and sprinkle with the Parmesan before serving.

Roasted tomato soup

This is the brainchild of Darren, one of Marcus Wareing's chefs at Petrus, and is so good that we've all stolen it! It's a great way of using up tomatoes that are on the turn, and a touch of cream can be added to lighten the flavour if it's a little intense. You can buy smoked tomatoes from good delicatessens. Serve cold or hot with crostini (page 229).

Serves 4–6
1.5 kg overripe tomatoes
200 g sun-dried tomatoes
50 g smoked tomatoes
1 celery stick, cut into 6
1 head of garlic, split in half horizontally
5 sprigs of fresh thyme
1 bunch of fresh basil stalks
1 bunch of fresh parsley stalks
100 ml olive oil
400–500 ml Vegetable stock (page 261)
rock salt and freshly ground black pepper

To serve
12 cherry tomatoes, halved
handful of fresh basil leaves, roughly torn
olive oil, for drizzling

Preheat the oven to 200°C/Gas Mark 6. Place a large roasting tin in the oven.

In a large bowl mix all the tomatoes together with the celery, garlic, thyme and herb stalks. Season with a good sprinkling of rock salt.

When the baking tin begins to smoke, add the olive oil. Then add the tomato mixture and roast in the oven for 20–30 minutes, or until the tomatoes begin to blister. Make sure you stir occasionally to prevent anything burning.

Transfer the mixture to a large bowl, cover with cling film and leave to marinate for 1 hour.

Add enough vegetable stock to cover, then blitz the whole lot in a blender or food processor. If the soup seems too thick, add a little more stock. Transfer the soup to a pan, season to taste and warm through gently.

Prepare the garnish by combining the cherry tomatoes and basil with a drizzle of olive oil and a little rock salt.

Pour the soup into individual bowls, top each one with some garnish and add a final drizzle of olive oil.

Fennel soup

This is like vichyssoise, but uses fennel instead of leeks. You could serve with some finely sliced fennel on top, or a sprinkling of chopped dill. If you're feeling extravagant, fry up the fennel and deglaze the pan with a little Pernod.

Serves 4
4 tbsp olive oil
5 fennel bulbs, trimmed and
roughly chopped
500 ml Vegetable stock (page 261)
100 ml double cream
salt and freshly ground black pepper

Heat the oil in a large pan over a medium heat. Season the fennel and add to the pan. Cook for 10–15 minutes, until the fennel starts to soften but doesn't colour.

Add the stock and bring to the boil. Reduce the heat and simmer for 10 minutes, or until the fennel is soft and cooked through. Remove from the heat and allow to cool a little before blitzing in a food processor or blender.

Pass the mixture through a sieve and return to the pan. Stir in the cream. Taste and adjust the seasoning, and then reheat until piping hot before serving.

Meat broth

Nonna always used to have broth in the fridge to use as a base for soups and stews. She took so much time and care making it that it was always crystal clear. While chicken is the base of this recipe, a bit of brisket, pancetta and sausage are added – I know this seems like a lot of meat to use just for a broth, but it's vital for the depth of flavour that's needed here. If you like, you can reserve the cooked meats and serve them cold. This broth is used for Anolini (page 76), or you can serve it as a soup with ditalini (small pasta shapes).

Serves 4
200 g beef brisket
100 g smoked bacon (Alsace if you can find it) or pancetta, in one piece
1 Toulouse sausage, about 50 g
1 x 1.5 kg free-range chicken, jointed into 8–10 pieces
1 onion, chopped
1 celery stick, chopped
1 leek, chopped
1 carrot, chopped
1 head of garlic, cut in half horizontally
1 sprig of fresh thyme
1 bay leaf
salt and freshly ground black pepper

Cut the brisket, bacon and sausage into large chunks about the same size as the chicken pieces.

Put the chopped meat and the chicken into a large pan and cover with cold water. Bring to the boil, then reduce the heat and simmer for 1 hour, skimming off any scum as frequently as possible.

When the meat has cooked for 1 hour, add the remaining ingredients, then simmer for a further 1–1 ½ hours. Continue to taste and season until you feel the flavour is right.

Strain the liquid through a sieve into a clean pan and discard the meat. Check the seasoning and reheat before serving in individual bowls.

Fish soup

In the area where the Italian and French coastlines meet, you get the most fantastic fish soups. Ligurian fish soup is the Italian classic, while further along the coast is the French classic, bouillabaisse. You can put any fish or seafood you like into it – prawns, squid, mussels and clams are usually included – and the whole dish is finished simply with parsley and tomato. This soup does involve a lot of preparation, but once you add the fish, it cooks quickly and every mouthful is worth the effort.

Serves 4

100 ml olive oil, plus extra for drizzling
2 banana shallots or 3 ordinary shallots, finely sliced
4 garlic cloves, crushed
1 tsp finely chopped fresh red chilli
20 mussels or clams, scrubbed and beards removed
200 ml white wine
8 large raw king prawns or langoustines, heads and shells removed
200 g small pasta, e.g. ditalini or fregola
250 ml Fish stock (page 259) or water
200 g monkfish, cut into bite-sized pieces
2 sea bream or baby bass fillets, about 350 g each, cut into bite-sized pieces
4 red mullet fillets, about 100 g each
4 tbsp Basic tomato sauce (page 256)
1 tbsp chopped fresh flatleaf parsley

Heat the olive oil in a large pan over a medium heat. Add the shallots, garlic and chilli and cook gently, until soft but not coloured – about 2 minutes.

Turn up the heat, add the cleaned mussels or clams and pour in the wine. Cover with a lid and cook for 4–5 minutes, or until all the mussels or clams are open. Discard any that remain closed. Drain the stock into a bowl and set aside.

Pick the mussels or clams from their shells, leaving about 8 in the shell for presentation. Set aside.

Make a shallow incision along the back of each langoustine or prawn, then use the tip of the knife to pull out the black intestinal tract. This should be discarded. Set aside.

Bring a pan of salted water to the boil. Add the pasta and boil for about 4 minutes, or until *al dente*. Drain and cool in iced water. Add a touch of olive oil to prevent the pasta sticking together, and set aside.

Heat a wide, deep frying pan and add the mussel or clam stock and fish stock. Bring to a very gentle simmer; the bubbles should be barely breaking the surface. Add the monkfish, prawns or langoustines, and sea bream or bass, and poach lightly for 3 minutes. Add the red mullet and cook for a further 3 minutes. Now add the tomato sauce and the cooked mussels or clams, stirring lightly so that they just heat through. Stir in the drained pasta and the parsley, and finish with a generous drizzle of olive oil. Garnish with the reserved mussels before serving.

Starters

The starter is my favourite part of any meal. Even when I eat in Indian and Chinese restaurants, I prefer to have a selection of starters rather than a main course. In Italian cuisine, the world of antipasti is vast and versatile. Traditionally, a basket of bread is served, then the antipasti, pasta, main course and dessert or cheese. This is why people often think Italian food is filling – but really it's because they stuff themselves as soon as they sit down and are then too full to eat the rest of the meal. It's understandable: antipasti are so appetizing that it's difficult to stop at one, and you can easily go on to nibble three or four.

Antipasti in Emilia-Romagna would usually be a plate of salami, prosciutto or coppa, plus a selection of small vegetarian starters. (Being in the mountains, it's rare to find any fish on the menu.) At the Connaught I still like to serve a plate of prosciutto with melon at the beginning of our multi-course tasting menu. For a casual dinner at home, I'll include ingredients such as olives, pickles and peppers stuffed with goat's cheese (see Snacks, page 222).

This chapter offers a selection of traditional starters from all over Italy. Most of the meat dishes hail from Emilia-Romagna, such as the delicious Deep-fried pasta with culatello (page 47), and the rest are my own takes on classic starters, such as Grilled asparagus with fried duck eggs (page 44). I've also included a traditional speciality of my grandmother's – Stuffed onions with Parmesan breadcrumbs (page 41).

Starters should, by their very nature, be appetizing and make you want to eat more: their job is to get your tastebuds going and awaken your appetite. To achieve this, always choose ingredients that are in season – don't try making the Ricotta and spring vegetable salad (page 38), for example, in midwinter. In addition, always make sure your starter balances well with your main course or pasta dish. This means not doing a fish starter and fish main; instead, offer perhaps a beef carpaccio followed by a lightly grilled piece of fish. In fact, I tend to prefer things the other way round, with fish as the starter and meat for the main course, but either way, you'll find lots of delicious ideas here.

Ricotta and spring vegetable salad

In southern Italy they have firm, salted ricotta, which is grated over salads and pasta like Parmesan, but I like the cool, soft ricotta in this salad against the crunch of the spring vegetables. You could also use goat's cheese, and whatever vegetables are available.

Serves 4
6–8 asparagus spears, trimmed
4 baby fennel or 1 fennel bulb, sliced into 4
250 g green beans, topped
100 g fresh peas
100 g broad beans
2 baby or small chicory heads, cut into quarters
150–200 g fresh ricotta

For the vinaigrette
250 ml olive oil
50 ml Cabernet Sauvignon or other red wine vinegar
salt and freshly ground black pepper

Bring a large pan of salted water to the boil. Add the fennel and cook for 3 minutes. Then add the asparagus for a further 2 minutes, followed by the green beans, peas and broad beans for another 3 minutes. Drain and refresh immediately in cold water.

Put the chicory and blanched vegetables into a large bowl and mix together.

To make the vinaigrette, whisk together the oil, wine vinegar and seasoning to taste. Add about three-quarters of the vinaigrette to the vegetables and toss to combine.

Divide the salad between four individual bowls and evenly distribute small teaspoons of ricotta over and around the salad. Finish by drizzling over the remaining vinaigrette.

Stuffed onions with Parmesan breadcrumbs

This is a phenomenal dish that my grandmother used to make – definitely one of my all-time favourites. It's delicious on its own or with a crisp green salad. I can't promise that mine is as good as hers, but it's pretty tasty all the same.

Serves 4
4 medium onions, peeled and left whole
100 g fresh white breadcrumbs
100 g Parmesan, freshly grated
4 tbsp chopped fresh flatleaf parsley
olive oil, for drizzling
Chicken stock (page 260) or water, if needed
salt and freshly ground black pepper

For the sauce
10 g dried porcini mushrooms, soaked in about 250 ml hot water for 5 minutes
2 tbsp olive oil
2 knobs of butter
2 shallots, finely chopped
1 carrot, cut into 3 mm dice
1 celery stick, cut into 3 mm dice
1 tsp tomato purée
splash of red wine

Drain the soaked porcini, reserving the liquid.

To make the sauce, heat the oil and 1 knob of butter in a pan. Add the shallots, carrot and celery and cook until soft and translucent, about 3–4 minutes. Add the drained mushrooms and the remaining knob of butter and continue to cook for a further 2–3 minutes.

Add the tomato purée and cook, stirring constantly, for another minute. Add a splash of red wine and bubble until completely reduced. Finally, add the strained mushroom liquid, reduce the heat and simmer for 45 minutes to 1 hour until it has formed a thick, sauce-like consistency.

Preheat the oven to 200°C/Gas Mark 6.

Meanwhile, bring a large pan of salted water to the boil, add the onions and boil for 3 minutes. Remove and drain. Cut each onion in half and scoop out the centre with a spoon, leaving 2–3 layers intact round the outside, and setting the onion flesh aside. This will leave you with 8 onion shells.

Finely chop the scooped-out onion and place in a bowl. Mix in the breadcrumbs, Parmesan and enough of the reduced mushroom sauce to bind the mixture together (about a tablespoon). Stir in the parsley and season to taste.

Put the onion shells in an ovenproof dish and drizzle with olive oil. Fill each shell with the stuffing and top with the mushroom sauce. Cover with foil and bake in the oven for 15–20 minutes. If the onions look dry at any point, sprinkle a little chicken stock or water over them. Remove and serve at once.

Opposite
Nonna, *c.* 1920

Deep-fried vegetables with aïoli

Aïoli is a traditional French garlic mayonnaise, a fantastic accompaniment to crispy fried vegetables. If made properly in a light, Japanese-style tempura batter and drained well, deep-fried vegetables are not at all greasy. You can serve them as a starter, or alongside a main course, such as Baked baby sea bass (page 124).

Serves 4
selection of summer vegetables
e.g. 1 red pepper, 1 yellow pepper,
1 small aubergine, 2 courgettes,
6 asparagus spears, 4 baby fennel bulbs
vegetable oil, for deep-frying
100 g tempura flour
150 ml ice-cold sparkling mineral water
100 g '00' flour, for dusting
10 fresh flatleaf parsley leaves

For the aïoli
2 small new potatoes
2 small garlic cloves, chopped
1 egg yolk
100 ml olive oil
salt and freshly ground black pepper

First make the aïoli. Bring a small pan of salted water to the boil and cook the new potatoes for 15 minutes, or until soft when pierced with the tip of a knife. Drain and set aside until cool enough for you to handle, but still quite hot.

Peel the potatoes and put them in a food processor with the garlic and egg yolk. Blitz briefly to blend, then, with the motor running, begin to add the olive oil, first in drops and then in a gradual stream. If the worst happens and the mixture curdles, add a few drops of boiling water to bring it back together. Once you've added about half the olive oil, the mixture should look like mayonnaise, and you can add the rest of the oil more quickly. You should end up with a thick, glossy, garlicky aïoli. Taste for seasoning and set aside until needed.

Prepare the vegetables for deep-frying. Seed the peppers and cut into eighths. Discard the centres of the aubergine and courgettes – you want just the skin and a little flesh; cut into large pieces about 6 cm long and 3 cm across. Cut the asparagus in half and the baby fennel into quarters.

Preheat a deep-fat fryer or a large pan of oil to 180°C.

Put the tempura flour into a bowl and place it over another bowl filled with iced water. This helps to keep the batter mix cold, and therefore as light as possible. Slowly pour in the sparkling water and mix with chopsticks. There's no need to beat the batter – lumps are fine.

Put the '00' flour in a large dish and season it. Toss the vegetables and parsley leaves briefly in the seasoned flour, then plunge them straight into the batter. Lift out a few vegetables and lower them straight into the hot oil. It's best to do the frying in batches so as not to overload the pan and reduce the temperature of the oil. Fry until golden brown.

With a slotted or wire spoon, carefully remove the vegetables from the oil and drain on kitchen paper. Prepare the remaining vegetables in the same way, and serve immediately with the aïoli for dipping.

Grilled asparagus with fried duck eggs

You can't beat new-season English asparagus (available in May and June). I'm not a fan of the spindly sprue variety because I think you need a bit of body to the spears. If you can't get duck eggs, use free-range hen's eggs. Although in most respects this is not a very Italian dish, it does illustrate the essence of Italian cooking: simple produce cooked in season with little complication.

Serves 4
20 asparagus spears, trimmed
4 tbsp olive oil, plus extra for frying
and drizzling
knob of butter
4 duck eggs
salt and freshly ground black pepper
handful of Parmesan shavings, to serve

Season the asparagus, place in a bowl and add the olive oil. Set aside.

Heat a griddle pan until hot, then add the asparagus. Grill for 3–4 minutes, turning halfway through, until the asparagus can be easily pierced with the tip of a sharp knife. Transfer to a roasting tin and cover tightly with cling film: this will allow the asparagus to steam and finish cooking.

Heat the butter and a little olive oil in a non-stick frying pan. Fry the duck eggs for 3–4 minutes, or until cooked to your liking.

Transfer the asparagus to individual serving plates. Lightly season the duck eggs and place on top of the grilled asparagus. Scatter the Parmesan shavings on top and drizzle with a little olive oil, if liked.

Deep-fried pasta
with culatello

Culatello is a great delicacy of the Emilia-Romagna region. This succulent meat is cut from the thigh of the pig, but, unlike Parma ham, is a boneless piece. There are only about ten producers of culatello around Parma, and it's available only from October to March. Slice it thinly and serve with deep-fried pasta – the combination just melts on the tongue.

Serves 4–6
400 g 'oo' flour
1 egg, beaten
3 tbsp olive oil
20 slices culatello or Parma ham
corn oil, for deep-frying
salt

Mix the flour with 1 tbsp salt and tip on to a board or work surface. Make a well in the centre and pour in the egg and olive oil. Gradually work in the flour from the outside until the mixture forms a dough. Add a little water if necessary. Knead for about 5 minutes, until the dough is quite solid and smooth. Wrap in cling film and leave to rest in the fridge for at least 1 hour.

Heat the corn oil in a deep-fat fryer or heavy-based pan to 180°C. Meanwhile, remove the dough from the fridge and divide into four. Roll each piece into a rectangle about 8 x 20 cm, then cut each one widthways at 2 cm intervals so that you end up with 10 pasta strips measuring 2 x 8 cm.

Check that the oil is hot enough by dropping in one pasta strip – it should immediately puff up like a pillow. Cook the strips in batches of 4 or 5, turning occasionally while they crisp up, for 2–3 minutes. Remove with a slotted or wire spoon and drain on kitchen paper. Serve immediately with the culatello or Parma ham.

Red mullet with hazelnuts and fennel

This is a really refreshing starter, and a great way to eat red mullet. The crunchiness of the hazelnuts contrasts with the tender flesh, and the vinegar gives the whole dish a kick.

Serves 4
50 g butter
50 g hazelnuts, skinned
125 ml olive oil, plus 4 tbsp
25 ml hazelnut oil
30 ml white wine vinegar
8 baby or small fennel bulbs
8 red mullet fillets, cleaned and pin-boned
4 tsp chopped fresh basil (chopped at last minute)
salt and freshly ground black pepper

Heat the butter in a non-stick frying pan until bubbling. Add the hazelnuts and roast over a medium heat for 2–3 minutes, constantly shaking the pan to prevent them sticking. Remove and leave to cool. Chop the hazelnuts roughly and place in a bowl.

Add the 125 ml of olive oil, the hazelnut oil and wine vinegar to the hazelnuts. Mix well to combine and season to taste. Set aside.

Place the fennel in a bowl, season and add 2 tablespoons of olive oil. Heat a griddle pan until hot, add the fennel and grill for 7–8 minutes, turning halfway through until browned and tender. Remove from the heat and set aside.

Heat the remaining 2 tablespoons of olive oil in a non-stick frying pan over a medium heat. Add the fish fillets, skin-side down, shaking the pan to stop them sticking. Cook for 3 minutes until nicely browned, then turn gently using a palette knife. Cook for another 2 minutes, then remove from the pan.

Place two pieces of grilled fennel on each plate and top with two fish fillets. Spoon over a little hazelnut dressing and scatter basil over the top. Serve immediately.

Griddled sardines

With delicious fresh sardines, you shouldn't start messing around and doing anything fancy. The charry smell of the fish grilling, along with the zesty, lemony dressing, evoke memories of summer holidays on the beach in the Med.

Serves 4
8 fresh sardines, scaled and gutted
250 ml olive oil, plus extra for drizzling
50 ml red wine vinegar
100 g capers
juice of 1 lemon
2 tbsp chopped fresh flatleaf parsley
salt and freshly ground black pepper

Heat a griddle pan over a medium heat until very hot. If your pan isn't hot enough, the sardines will stick when you cook them.

Place the sardines in a shallow roasting tin or dish. Season well and drizzle over a little olive oil.

Make a vinaigrette by mixing the olive oil with the wine vinegar, capers, lemon juice, parsley and a little salt. Check the seasoning and set aside.

Place the sardines gently on the hot griddle pan and cook for at least 3–4 minutes before turning. (If you try to turn the sardines earlier, the skin will stick and tear.) Cook for another 3–4 minutes.

Remove from the pan and place on a serving dish. Liberally cover with the vinaigrette and serve immediately.

Vitello tonnato

Translated simply as 'veal and tuna', this Italian classic sounds rather unappetizing, but it's actually delicious. The chefs at the Connaught thought I was mad when I first suggested the combination! Make it 24 hours ahead and use very good-quality tuna in oil. Serve this as an antipasto or just with green salad or bread.

Serves 4
1 carrot, roughly chopped
1 small onion, roughly chopped
1 celery stick, roughly chopped
1 leek, roughly chopped
1 sprig of fresh thyme
1 bay leaf
500 g lean veal rump
handful of caperberries, to serve

For the tuna mayonnaise
2 large egg yolks
3 tbsp lemon juice
300 ml olive oil
5 anchovy fillets
200 g canned tuna
3 tbsp small capers
salt

Put all the vegetables and herbs in a large pan. Cover with water and bring to the boil. Add the veal, reduce the heat and cook for 45 minutes to 1 hour so that the meat is cooked but remains pink in the middle. Remove from the heat and allow the veal to cool in the cooking juices.

In a bowl, whisk the egg yolks with the lemon juice and a little salt. Gradually whisk in the olive oil a few drops at a time a first, then pour it in steadily in a thin stream until you have a thick and glossy mayonnaise.

Put the anchovies, tuna and capers in a food processor and blitz together. Fold this mixture into the mayonnaise.

Slice the veal thinly and place a layer of slices in a large, flat dish. Add a layer of the tuna sauce, then keep building alternate layers, finishing with a layer of sauce. Cover with cling film and refrigerate overnight.

When ready to serve, return the veal to room temperature and garnish with caperberries.

Mackerel with filo pastry

The mackerel needs to be extremely fresh and sliced incredibly thinly, as it's barely cooked when served. You can assemble these little open pastries ahead of time and pop in the oven later.

Serves 4
4 x 90 g fresh mackerel fillets, skinned and pin-boned
500 g vine-ripened tomatoes
100 g butter
7 sheets of filo pastry
olive oil, for drizzling
salt and freshly ground black pepper

Preheat the oven to 180°C/Gas Mark 4.

Slice each mackerel fillet into 6 thin pieces.

To prepare the tomatoes, make a little incision with a sharp knife in the top of each one. Bring a pan of salted water to the boil and blanch the tomatoes in it for 10 seconds. Drain and transfer immediately to a bowl of iced water – this will make the skins easier to remove. Peel, quarter and de-seed the tomatoes, then cut the flesh into 5 mm squares. Set aside.

Heat the butter in a small pan over a low heat, making sure it does not boil. Remove from the direct heat and leave to rest in a warm place on the hob for 10 minutes. At this point it should separate into three layers. Discard the bottom and top layers so you are left with clarified butter.

Lay a sheet of filo pastry on a baking sheet, keeping the rest of the pastry covered with a damp cloth to prevent it drying out. Brush with the clarified butter and top with another sheet of filo. Continue the process with the remaining 5 sheets, finishing with a plain sheet of filo. Bake in the preheated oven for 10 minutes, then set aside to cool.

Cut the pastry into four rectangles measuring about 10 x 6 cm. Scatter a quarter of the tomatoes over each piece and arrange the mackerel slices on top. Drizzle with a little olive oil, season and bake for 5–7 minutes, or until the fish is just cooked.

Gratinated clams on salt

Stuart Gillies at the Boxwood Café in London serves clams this way, on a big bed of rock salt. It's quite easy, but looks incredibly impressive at a dinner party. Adding Parmesan or Gruyère to the crust brings it all together in one melting and sticky whole. If you get small clams, you'll need to increase the quantity to 40–45 to feed four. It's worth buying a few more clams in case you have to discard any that don't open.

Serves 4
2 tbsp olive oil
2 shallots, finely sliced
25–30 large Palourde clams in their shells, scrubbed
50 ml white wine
500 g rock salt, to serve

For the topping
50 g stale white breadcrumbs
2 tbsp finely chopped mixed fresh herbs, e.g. parsley, basil, thyme, rosemary
1 garlic clove, finely chopped
4 tbsp olive oil
50 g Parmesan or Gruyère, freshly grated

Start by making the topping. In a bowl mix the breadcrumbs with the herbs, garlic, olive oil and cheese; the texture should be dry enough to sprinkle. Set aside.

Now prepare the clams. Place the olive oil in a heavy-based pan over a medium heat. When hot, add the shallots and cook for 2–3 minutes, or until soft.

Add the clams and wine, cover with a lid and cook for 4–5 minutes, or until the shells open. Remove the clams from the pan and drain the juices into a bowl. Set aside.

Discard any clams that have not opened. Remove the top shell from each clam, leaving the meat in the lower shell. Transfer to a baking sheet and sprinkle with the herb topping.

Cook the clams under a hot grill until the topping is golden brown and starting to bubble.

Serve on a bed of rock salt and drizzle over a little of the reserved clam juices.

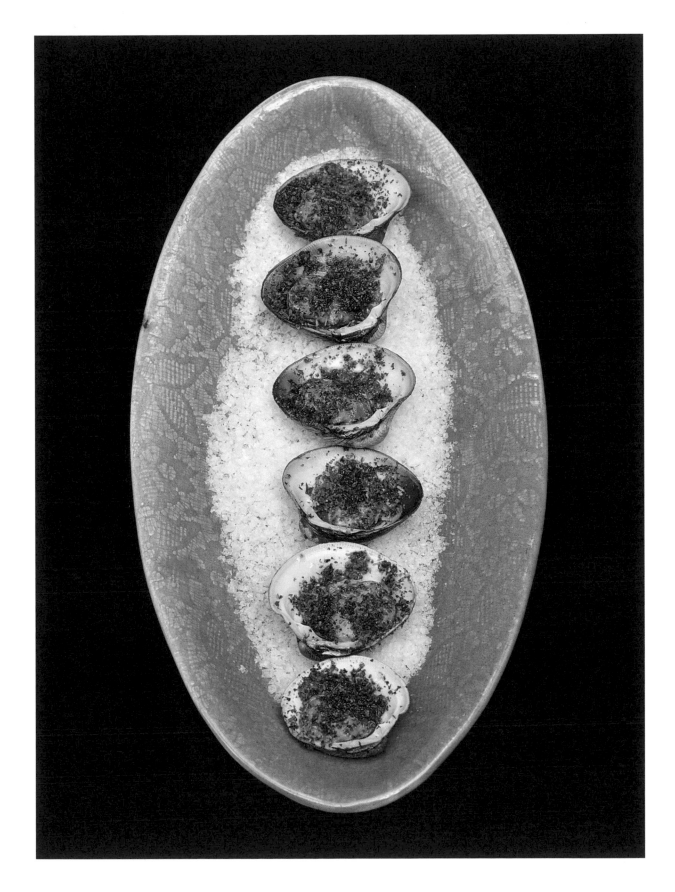

Carpaccio of beef

Carpaccio (usually very thinly sliced meat or fish, though you can make a carpaccio of vegetables too) doesn't have to be a posh restaurant dish – it's actually quite straightforward. The secret is to freeze it first, and then it slices easily. Make sure you use only the freshest, best-quality beef you can buy.

Serves 4
500 g piece of beef fillet
24 asparagus spears
4 tbsp olive oil, plus extra for drizzling
handful of Parmesan shavings
salt and freshly ground black pepper

Prepare the beef by trimming off any excess fat. Place it on a large piece of cling film and roll it up tightly into a cylinder shape about 6 cm in diameter. Make sure the beef is tied securely at both ends. Transfer to the freezer and leave overnight.

When ready to serve the next day, heat a griddle pan over a medium heat. Brush the asparagus spears with the olive oil, season and then grill for 4 minutes, turning halfway through. They should be only partly cooked. Transfer to a plate and cover tightly with cling film. This will allow the asparagus to steam and cook through until tender.

Remove the beef from the freezer, take off the cling film and leave for 10 minutes to thaw slightly. With a razor-sharp knife, carve paper-thin slices of beef. Place enough slices on each serving plate to completely cover the interior.

When all the plates of beef are prepared, season with salt and pepper and drizzle over a little olive oil. Finish with the grilled asparagus and some Parmesan shavings on top.

Pasta and Grains

One of my ultimate food heroines is the great Italian–American cookery writer, Marcella Hazan. In *The Second Classic Italian Cookbook*, she had some words of wisdom: 'Pasta can be one of the easiest dishes in the world to prepare. It is also one of the easiest to ruin.'

This is so true. My friend John always hated pasta for the simple reason that he disliked the idea of eating bowl after bowl of the same thing. Needless to say, he had only ever eaten bad pasta. Once I cooked him the real thing, I convinced him instantly, and now he loves it. When I was studying at college, I found the same problem among my friends. All the 'Italian' meals they cooked were bastardized versions of classic dishes, the worst culprit being spaghetti Bolognese, with minced beef and even chilli. To add to the horror I felt, it would be served with pre-grated Parmesan. What a snob I was! I slowly introduced them to freshly grated Parmesan and properly cooked pasta.It's a wonder I left university with any friends. But I suppose it just depends on what you're used to. I was lucky that I'd grown up eating the real thing and watching my grandmother and mother making the pasta. However, it was my time with Giorgio Locatelli at Zafferano that showed me how to implement that knowledge in a restaurant environment.

We have two specialities in our family village of Bardi – anolini and tortelli de erbetta – and I have spent many summers going from one local restaurant to another to see who has made the best that year. Anolini are filled pasta shapes that float in a rich, meaty broth (page 76). We can spend hours making them, but it's a tradition that brings us together as a family. Tortelli are the classic spinach and ricotta parcels, and it's incredible how differently people make them according to where they live. In our village they contain lots of spinach, while the nearer one goes to Parma, the bigger they become and the more ricotta they contain.

I've also given recipes for risotto, gnocchi and polenta in this chapter. Like pasta, these are dishes that vary hugely, depending on where you are in Italy. Eat a risotto in the Veneto area and it will be like soup; in Emilia-Romagna it's much drier. Polenta and gnocchi are both from northern Italy, where most of the maize is grown. People tend either to love or hate polenta; I absolutely love it. During the summer I spent at Nonna's when I sulked for two weeks (see page 18), I refused to come out of my room for dinner one night, even though my second cousin Maria had made polenta with rabbit and mushroom ragù. My Uncle Jonas still tells me to this day how I missed out on the best meal ever!

Pasta dough

Italy is the true home of pasta, though some historians would have us believe that it comes originally from China. The most important thing is that Italians have made it their own, and that every region has its specialities. In Emilia-Romagna we worship pasta, and the dishes have a real richness to them, with plenty of Parmesan and meat. We also use lots of different shapes, from ravioli to lasagne, and tortellini to spaghetti.

It was my grandmother who taught me how to make pasta. We'd pour a heap of flour on to the work surface and make a well in the centre; then we'd crack the eggs into a bowl, add a touch of olive oil, and mix together before pouring the liquid into the well and working it together. If more liquid was needed, we'd add a little warm water. It was all done by hand – mainly Nonna's, I must admit. (My later attempt to persuade Nonna to make pasta in a food processor was dismissed with contempt: even at eighty years old, she was stronger than me.) Nothing was weighed – all the ingredients were down to judgement. Then we would each take a turn at kneading. Only as I got older did I weigh out my pasta ingredients so that I had some idea of a recipe.

Makes 600 g
400 g '00' pasta flour
½ tsp salt
4 eggs
1 tbsp olive oil

Mix the flour and salt together and tip on to a work surface or board. Make a well in the centre.

Mix together the eggs and oil and pour two-thirds into the well, reserving the rest. Starting from the outside, work the flour into the liquid until a dough forms. The dough is conditioned by its environment, so depending on the warmth of your kitchen and hands, you may need to add the remaining egg mixture if the dough doesn't come together. Knead until it is smooth, firm and elastic (this will take 5–10 minutes). Wrap in cling film and rest in the fridge for 1 hour before using. The dough will keep for up to 24 hours in the fridge if wrapped tightly first in cling film and then in foil.

Rolling out the dough

Cut the dough into 3–4 pieces and use a rolling pin or the palm of your hand to flatten a piece to the width of your pasta machine. Make sure your pasta machine is on its widest setting, and run each piece of dough through it twice. Reduce the setting by one notch and run it through twice again. If the dough feels a bit sticky, add a little flour, but not too much, as this will dry it out.

Run it through the machine twice on each notch until you get to the narrowest or second narrowest notch, depending on the type of pasta you are making (see below). Halfway through this process you will need to fold the dough in half before finishing rolling.

Anolini

Roll the dough as described above and then run it twice through the narrowest notch. Cut into a long strip 10 cm wide. Put two-thirds of a teaspoon of filling at intervals along the strip, about 2.5 cm apart and two thirds of the way down the strip. Brush between and around each mound of filling with egg wash (a little beaten egg and water). Fold over the long side of the pasta nearest to you so that it completely covers the filling. Cup your hand and carefully press down around each mound to get all the air out. Using a 3–4 cm cutter or shot glass, cut out individual rounds.

Pappardelle

Roll the dough as described above and then run it twice through the last but one notch. Using a serrated pastry wheel, cut it into strips about 3 x 20 cm. You should end up with lots of crinkly ribbons. Drape flat over a rolling pin to dry out for 20 minutes before use (you can leave the papardelle to dry for up to 1 hour, but the pasta becomes more brittle the longer it is left). You need about 6–8 strips of pappardelle per starter portion, 8–10 for a main course.

Ravioli

Roll the dough as described above and then run it twice through the narrowest notch. Using a round 9 cm cutter, cut out circles of pasta. Place a dessertspoon of filling in the centre of half the circles. Brush egg wash around the filling, then place a disc of pasta on top. Quickly press all the way round with your thumb and first finger, pushing out all the air. Don't handle the pasta too much or it will become soft and sticky. Use the cutter or scissors to neaten up the edges.

Tagliatelle

Roll the dough as described above and then run it twice through the last but one notch. Your sheet of pasta should be about 30 cm in length. To cut into tagliatelle, use the attachment that comes with the machine. Sprinkle the dough with a little flour before running it through, catching the ribbons over your arm as they come out of the other side. Divide the ribbons in half and form into little nests – each nest is

about enough for one person as a starter portion. Set aside to dry out for 20 minutes before use (you can leave the tagliatelle to dry for up to 1 hour, but the pasta becomes more brittle the longer it is left).

If you don't have the tagliatelle attachment, simply roll up the pasta into a pinwheel and, using a sharp knife, slice into strips 8–10 mm thick. Separate the ribbons and form nests, as above.

Tortelli

Roll the dough as described on page 62 and then run it twice through the narrowest notch. Using a serrated pastry wheel, cut into a long strip 10 cm wide. Put 1 heaped teaspoon of filling at intervals along the strip, about 2.5 cm apart and two-thirds of the way down the strip (see photo opposite). Brush in between each mound of filling with egg wash. Fold over the long side of pasta nearest to you. Cup your hand and carefully press down around each mound to get all the air out. Brush the top third of the strip with egg wash and fold it back down over the mounds, again pressing down with your cupped hand. Using a serrated pastry wheel, cut out individual tortelli.

Key points for cooking pasta

• The water must be seasoned well with plenty of salt at the point when it comes to the boil – allow about 1 tablespoon of salt for a large pan of water.
• All the pasta must be covered with water.
• Stir the pasta when it first goes into the water and then leave alone.
• Always cook it to the point where it becomes *al dente.*
• Drain it well.

A pet hate of mine is when people cook the pasta in boiling water, but then drain and rinse it under cold water, washing off the starch. The starch is what allows the pasta and sauce to amalgamate. But the worst sin of all is to serve the pasta straight into a bowl and spoon the sauce on without mixing it in. Follow the recipes in this chapter and you can't go far wrong.

Tagliatelle with summer truffle

Truffles aren't really about taste – it's their unique, earthy scent that makes them so special. The best are gathered in the winter, but since just a small one could cost up to £80, why not try the more economical summer variety, as used in this recipe?

Serves 4

1 quantity Pasta dough (page 61)
150 g butter
100 ml Vegetable or Chicken stock (pages 260–1)
30 g summer truffle, very finely sliced
salt and freshly ground black pepper

Roll out the pasta and cut into tagliatelle as described on page 62. Set aside.

Put the butter and stock in a small pan over a low heat. When the butter has melted, whisk to form a sauce. Remove from the heat and set aside.

Bring a large pan of salted water to the boil. Add the tagliatelle and cook for 3–4 minutes, until *al dente*. Drain well, then toss with the butter sauce. Season to taste and serve immediately, topped with the truffle slices.

Tagliatelle with peas and Parma ham

This is a great, simple dish, perfect in the summer when fresh peas are in season. If you're vegetarian, use goat's cheese or ricotta instead of Parma ham.

Serves 4
1 quantity Pasta dough (page 61)
200 g fresh peas, podded weight
50 ml olive oil, plus extra for drizzling
1 garlic clove, crushed
handful freshly chopped mint
handful freshly grated Parmesan
8 slices Parma ham or 200 g soft goat's cheese, crumbled
salt and freshly ground black pepper

Roll out the pasta and cut into tagliatelle as described on page 62. Set aside.

Bring a medium pan of salted water to the boil. Add the peas and cook for 2–3 minutes. Drain and plunge into iced water. Set aside.

Heat the olive oil in a pan over a low heat and add the garlic. Cook for 1 minute, then add the drained peas and cook for a further 2–3 minutes. Remove from the heat and set aside.

Bring a large pan of salted water to the boil and cook the tagliatelle for 3–4 minutes, until *al dente*.

Drain and add to the pea mixture. Toss well, then season to taste and add the chopped mint and a drizzle of olive oil. Sprinkle in the Parmesan and drape over the Parma ham or scatter with the goat's cheese before serving.

Rabbit pappardelle

This is a very rustic creation from Emilia-Romagna, and in my view there's no tastier pasta dish in Italy. The rabbit is slowly roasted, then stewed to make the most fantastic, rich meat sauce, and it's served with wide ribbon noodles called pappardelle. If you want to make this with a whole rabbit, remember that some parts will cook more quickly than others; I find it easier just to roast a few legs.

Serves 4–6
1 quantity Pasta dough (page 61)
4 rabbit legs
50 ml olive oil
knob of butter
1 small carrot, finely chopped
1 small onion, finely chopped
1 celery stick, finely chopped
2 garlic cloves, crushed
2 sprigs fresh thyme
2 sprigs fresh rosemary
1 tsp tomato purée
½ glass white wine
about 250 ml Chicken or Vegetable stock
(pages 260–1)
salt and freshly ground black pepper
freshly grated Parmesan, to serve
small handful freshly chopped flatleaf
parsley, to serve

Cut the pasta into pappardelle (see page 62) and set aside until ready to cook.

Meanwhile, season the rabbit legs. Heat the olive oil and butter in a pan, add the rabbit legs and brown on all sides.

Remove the rabbit from the pan, add the vegetables, garlic and herbs and cook for 4–5 minutes, or until evenly coloured.

Return the rabbit legs to the pan and add the tomato purée. Cook for 2 minutes, then add the wine and turn up the heat to bubble and reduce.

Pour over enough stock to cover, then place a cartouche (a circle of baking parchment) on top and cook on a low simmer until the meat comes away easily from the bones. This will take about 45 minutes. Remove the rabbit and set aside until cool enough to handle. Lightly shred the meat into small pieces. Discard the bones.

Strain the stock, discarding the vegetables, and return to a clean pan. Add the rabbit pieces to the stock and place over a medium heat. Simmer until reduced and thick.

Bring a large pan of salted water to the boil and cook the pappardelle for 4–5 minutes, or until *al dente*. Drain and toss with the rabbit sauce. Serve scattered with the freshly grated Parmesan and chopped parsley.

Spinach and ricotta tortelli

This is a regional speciality of Emilia-Romagna; from Parma to Bologna, everyone makes it. You can buy ready-made spinach tortelli in British supermarkets, but once you've had the genuine article, there's no going back. You need good-quality, fresh ricotta rather than the stuff in a tub – Sairass ricotta, available from good delicatessens and cheese shops, is my favourite.

Serves 4
400 g spinach
150 g ricotta
pinch of grated nutmeg
50 g fresh breadcrumbs
75 g Parmesan, freshly grated, plus extra to serve
1 quantity Pasta dough (page 61)
olive oil, for drizzling
salt and freshly ground black pepper

Heat the spinach in a large pan with 2 tablespoons of water until it wilts down, about 3 minutes. Remove and set aside to cool. Once cold, squeeze out all the excess moisture. Chop the spinach finely and place in a bowl.

Add the ricotta to the spinach and mix together. Add the nutmeg, breadcrumbs and Parmesan and season to taste. Refrigerate until you're ready to fill the tortelli.

Roll out the pasta dough and make the tortelli as described on page 65, using ¾ teaspoon of filling per tortelli.

At this stage you can par-cook them to use later. Bring a large pan of salted water to the boil and blanch the tortelli in it for 30 seconds. Drain and plunge immediately into iced water. Remove and place on a lightly oiled baking sheet. Drizzle with a little olive oil and then cover with cling film. The tortelli can be refrigerated for up to 24 hours.

When ready to cook, boil the tortelli in a large pan of salted water for 3 minutes. Drain and serve immediately with a drizzle of olive oil and extra Parmesan.

Pumpkin tortelli

While pumpkin tortelli are a speciality of Mantua in Lombardy, these little stuffed parcels are also popular in Emilia-Romagna. Sometimes after boiling, the tortelli are fried in butter and then deglazed in amaretto liqueur, but they are delicious just boiled and drizzled with sage butter. If you can't get hold of pumpkin, use butternut squash or sweet potato instead.

Serves 4–6
½ pumpkin (about 2 kg), seeded and cut into wedges
100 g Parmesan, freshly grated
100 g Mustard fruits, chopped (page 250)
1 quantity Pasta dough (page 61)
2–3 amaretti biscuits, crushed
salt and freshly ground black pepper

For the sage butter
200 ml Vegetable stock (page 261)
100 g butter
12 fresh sage leaves

Start this recipe the day before you want to eat it.

Preheat the oven to 180°C/Gas Mark 4. Arrange the pumpkin wedges in a roasting tin and sprinkle with rock salt. Cover the tin with foil and cook in the oven for 45–50 minutes, or until tender when pierced with the point of a knife. Remove from the oven, allow to cool enough to handle, then scrape the pumpkin flesh from the skin. Place the flesh in a muslin cloth or a fine sieve and hang overnight above a bowl in a cool place to drain off all the excess liquid.

Place the pumpkin in a food processor and blend until smooth. Add the Parmesan and mustard fruits and season. Pulse-blend to combine.

Roll out and cut up the pasta dough as described on page 65. Place 1 teaspoon of filling at 2 cm intervals along each strip of pasta, then fold into parcels about 3 cm square (see page 65).

At this stage you can par-cook them to use later. Bring a large pan of salted water to the boil and blanch the tortelli in it for 30 seconds. Drain and plunge immediately into iced water. Remove and place on a lightly oiled baking sheet. Drizzle with a little olive oil and then cover with cling film. The tortelli can be refrigerated for up to 24 hours.

Place the stock and butter in a pan and bring to the boil over a medium heat, whisking vigorously to stop the mixture splitting. Add the sage leaves and a little seasoning just before serving.

Bring a large pan of salted water to the boil. Add the tortelli and cook for 3 minutes. Drain and serve, drizzled with the sage butter and with the amaretti crumbs sprinkled on top.

Anolini

Making anolini at Christmas is a long-standing tradition in my family. In fact, these ravioli-type parcels, filled with a stuffing based on a veal and beef stew mixed with breadcrumbs and Parmesan, are made by everyone in Emilia-Romagna. I've been making them with the women in my family ever since I can remember, and I will probably continue to do so until the day I die. Even when I was at college, I always went home for our anolini session. We had such an efficient system (I would roll out the pasta and Nonna would fill it) that we could make as many as 600 in one hit. These days, although there are more people involved, production is much slower – I love my mum and Aunt Viviana, but they do like to chat!

I use my grandmother's traditional anolini stamp to cut them out, but you could easily use a fluted cutter or a shot glass instead. The quantities given overleaf are those we'd make at home, the idea being that you get at least two meals out of this recipe: the anolini in broth and then the cold, sliced meat to eat another day with chutney or mustard fruits (see pages 253 and 250). If you don't want to do this, simply halve the quantities.

Opposite
The three sisters:
Nonna, Great
Auntie Maria and
Great Auntie Rosina

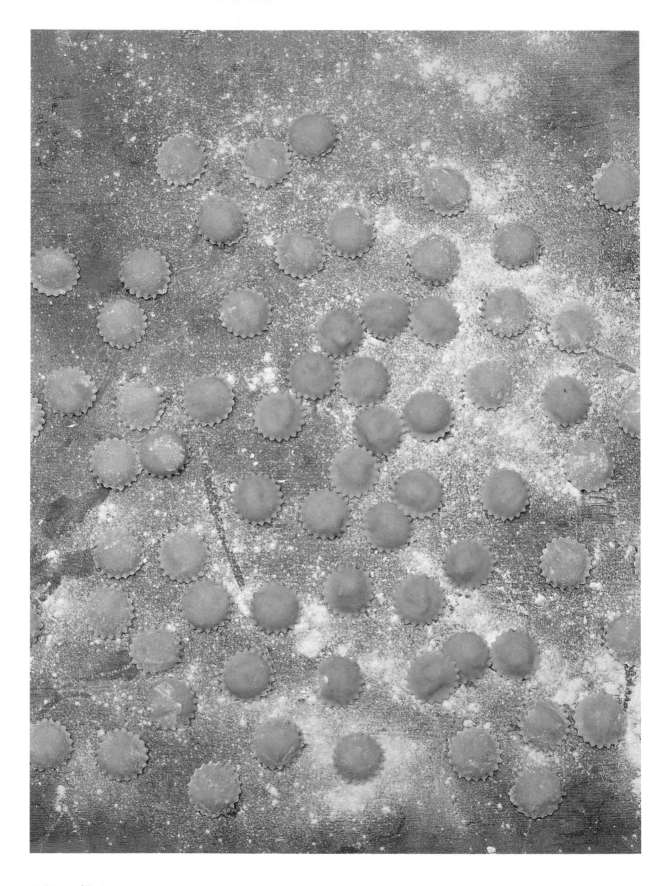

Serves 8–10 as a starter

100 ml olive oil

50 g butter

1 onion, roughly chopped

1 carrot, roughly chopped

1 celery stick, roughly chopped

1 leek, roughly chopped

leaves from 2 sprigs of fresh thyme

1.5 kg chuck beef, in one piece

500 g veal rump, in one piece

120 g Italian sausage (I like Lugano, but use anything slightly spicy)

2 tbsp tomato purée

a good splash of red or white wine

800 ml–1 litre Chicken stock (page 260)

200 g freshly grated Parmesan, plus extra to serve

100 g stale white breadcrumbs

1 quantity Pasta dough (page 61)

1 quantity Meat broth (page 33)

salt and freshly ground black pepper

Heat the olive oil and butter in a large pan over a medium heat. Add the onion, carrot, celery, leek and thyme leaves and cook gently, stirring occasionally, until soft and caramelized, about 5–10 minutes. Remove the vegetables from the pan and set aside.

Add the beef and cook on all sides until browned, about 5 minutes. Add the veal and sausage and continue to brown for another 10 minutes. Return the vegetables to the pan, add the tomato purée and cook for a further 2 minutes. Add the wine and allow it to bubble and reduce completely. Stir, then pour over enough chicken stock to completely cover the meat. Place a cartouche (a circle of baking parchment) over the mixture, reduce the heat to as low as possible, and cook gently for 2½–3 hours, stirring occasionally. The meat should be soft enough to cut with a spoon.

Remove the meat from the pan and set aside, reserving the juices. Allow to cool, then refrigerate until completely cold, before cutting half the meat into 5 mm dice. Set aside for the anolini filling. You can slice the rest of the meat and serve it cold.

To make the filling, put the Parmesan and breadcrumbs into a bowl and add enough of the reserved meat juices to form a soft paste. Add half the diced meat and mix well. Check the seasoning and refrigerate until ready to use. You can serve the remaining meat cold (see introduction).

Roll out the pasta dough and make the anolini according to the instructions on page 62.

Place the meat broth in a large pan and bring to the boil. Tip in the anolini and cook until they rise to the surface, about 3–4 minutes. Serve the broth and anolini in shallow dishes sprinkled with freshly grated Parmesan.

Crab linguine

You'll need the freshest possible crab meat for this. If you're feeling brave, you can buy a live crab and cook it yourself, but it's fine to get it precooked from your fishmonger. The key is to add it near the end to avoid overcooking. This dish is also lovely made with soft-shelled crab (page 111).

Serves 4
320 g dried linguine
2 tbsp olive oil
1 garlic clove, finely chopped
4 spring onions, finely chopped
½ tsp finely chopped fresh red chilli
300 g picked fresh white crab meat
25 ml dry white wine
1 tbsp chopped fresh flatleaf parsley
salt and freshly ground black pepper

Bring a large pan of salted water to the boil and cook the linguine for 7–8 minutes, or according to packet instructions, until *al dente*.

Meanwhile, heat the olive oil in a large, deep frying pan and add the garlic, spring onions and chilli. Fry lightly without colouring for 1 minute. Stir in the crab meat and heat through for another minute.

Add the wine to the pan and allow to bubble and reduce completely.

Drain the linguine and add to the crab mixture. Stir in the parsley and toss everything together to coat evenly. Season to taste and serve immediately.

Lobster spaghetti

When we put this on the menu at the Connaught, it was an instant bestseller. In fact, if we take it off, we always get regular customers requesting it. Except for grilling (see page 114), this is undoubtedly the best way to eat lobster. Use very fresh tomatoes for the sauce, and have only a touch of it – you mustn't overwhelm the delicate lobster. Always use dried spaghetti for this dish – it has a better consistency and is less sticky than fresh pasta. My favourite brand is Latini, but it's very hard to find in the UK, so I usually end up using De Cecco, which is also great.

Serves 4

2 live lobsters, about 600–800 g each
300 g dried spaghetti
50 ml olive oil, plus extra for drizzling
2 fresh red chillies, finely chopped
2 garlic cloves, crushed
4 spring onions, finely chopped
3 tbsp white wine
4 large plum tomatoes, quartered, seeded and cut into 1 cm dice
2 tbsp chopped fresh flatleaf parsley
2 tbsp chopped fresh basil (chopped at last minute)
salt and freshly ground black pepper

Place the lobsters in the freezer for a couple of hours before you cook them. This will send them to sleep.

Bring a large pan of salted water to the boil and then drop in your lobsters. Cook for 6–8 minutes until the lobsters have turned bright red in colour. Remove and set aside to drain and cool a little.

To remove the meat from the lobster, first twist off each claw and leg joint. Using lobster crackers or the back of a heavy knife, crack the claw and then twist out the lobster meat. Peel off the shell to access all the meat inside. Next twist the tail from the body by bending it back. Squeeze the sides of the tail together until they crack, and then you should be able to pull out the tail meat in one go. Remove the dark vein running down the back of the tail. Cut the meat into bite-size pieces and set aside.

Bring a large pan of salted water to the boil and cook the pasta for 7–8 minutes, or according to packet instructions, until *al dente*.

Meanwhile, heat the olive oil in another large pan and add the chillies, garlic and spring onions. Season well and cook gently, stirring, for 1–2 minutes without colouring.

Add the lobster meat and then the wine. Add a little more seasoning, then allow the wine to bubble and reduce right down for 2–3 minutes. Don't cook for longer than this or the lobster will go rubbery.

Add the tomatoes, cook for 1 minute, then remove from the heat.

Drain the pasta and add to the sauce. Toss well, then stir in the herbs, season to taste and serve drizzled with olive oil.

Spaghetti alle vongole

In the United States I find that Italian food tends to be very spiced up, which is not really authentic. A hint of chilli is sometimes found in southern Italian dishes such as this, but it should not overpower the other flavours.

Serves 4
300–350 g dried spaghetti
2 tbsp olive oil, plus extra for drizzling
½ tsp de-seeded and finely sliced fresh red chilli
2 garlic cloves, finely sliced
500 g small clams, scrubbed
splash of white wine
2 tbsp finely chopped fresh flatleaf parsley
salt and freshly ground black pepper

Bring a large pan of salted water to the boil and cook the spaghetti for about 7–8 minutes, or according to packet instructions, until *al dente*.

Meanwhile, heat the olive oil in a large, deep frying pan over a medium heat. Add the chilli and garlic and cook for 3–4 minutes, or until soft but not coloured. Add the clams to the pan along with the wine. Cover and cook over a fairly high heat for 2–3 minutes, or until the clams open. Remove from the heat, then pick out and discard any clams that have not opened.

Drain the spaghetti and add to the clams. Stir in the parsley and drizzle over a touch of olive oil if it looks a bit dry. Season to taste and serve immediately.

Spaghetti with peperoncini and garlic

This very simple Italian standby can be quickly put together after a busy day at work because it uses just store-cupboard basics. Beware: the peperoncini can be very spicy.

Serves 2
240 g dried spaghetti
2–3 tbsp olive oil
1 garlic clove, finely sliced
2 peperoncini (dried red chillies), crushed
1–2 tbsp chopped fresh flatleaf parsley
salt and freshly ground black pepper
freshly grated Parmesan, to serve

Bring a large pan of salted water to the boil. Add the spaghetti and stir as it starts to cook. Boil for 7–8 minutes, or according to packet instructions, until the pasta is *al dente*.

Meanwhile, heat the olive oil in a large, deep frying pan, add the garlic and peperoncini and cook for 30 seconds, until soft, but without colouring. Remove from the heat and set aside.

Drain the cooked spaghetti and toss with the peperoncini and garlic.

Stir in the chopped parsley, season to taste and scatter with Parmesan before serving immediately.

Opposite:
The moustachioed man on the right is my great-grandfather, Bartolomeo, pictured here with his friend Liborio Cordani, in Italy in the early 1900s

Penne Bolognese

I used to wonder why Nonna would spend ages cutting up beef for Bolognese sauce, rather than using minced beef bought from the butcher. The answer is because it tastes so much better. Traditionally this is the way it's always made.

Serves 4
2 tbsp olive oil
2 celery sticks, finely chopped
2 carrots, finely chopped
½ onion, finely chopped
1 garlic clove, finely chopped
500 g chuck steak, finely diced
150 g veal rump, finely diced
3 tbsp tomato purée
100 ml white or red wine
300–500 ml water or Chicken stock
(page 260)
400 g dried penne
salt and freshly ground black pepper
handful of freshly grated Parmesan,
to serve

Heat the olive oil over a low heat in a heavy-based pan. When hot, add the vegetables and garlic and cook gently, stirring occasionally to prevent sticking, but do not allow to colour.

Add the diced meat and colour slightly for a minute or two.

Add the tomato purée and cook for 4–5 minutes. (This ensures it acts as a thickening agent and does not overpower the meat.)

Add the wine, turn up the heat a little and allow to bubble and reduce. Cover with the water or stock and stir well. Cover with a cartouche (a circle of baking parchment). A good Bolognese should cook for at least 3–4 hours over a very low heat, but check it every hour and give it a stir. If necessary, add a touch of water so it does not dry out. When cooked, it should have formed a lovely thick sauce.

Bring a large pan of salted water to the boil and cook the penne for 10 minutes or according to packet instructions, until *al dente*. Drain and add to the Bolognese, then season to taste and toss well. Serve sprinkled with Parmesan.

Rigatoni with tomato and pancetta

It's difficult to starve if you have pasta in the cupboard and water in which to cook it. This is another quick and cheerful supper: if you don't have any pancetta, use smoked bacon. You can also throw in a few fresh or frozen peas if you like.

Serves 4
500 g rigatoni
1 tbsp olive oil, plus extra for drizzling
200 g pancetta, diced
1 quantity Basic tomato sauce (page 256)
1 tbsp chopped fresh flatleaf parsley
handful of freshly grated Parmesan
salt and freshly ground black pepper

Bring a large pan of salted water to the boil and add the rigatoni. Reduce the heat and simmer for 10 minutes, or according to packet instructions, until *al dente*.

Heat the oil in a large frying pan over a medium heat. Add the pancetta and cook, tossing occasionally, until it is golden brown on all sides, about 3–4 minutes.

Add the tomato sauce to the pancetta, reduce the heat and simmer gently for 2–3 minutes.

Drain the rigatoni and add it to the tomato sauce. Check the seasoning and adjust if necessary. Stir in the parsley and serve immediately with Parmesan and a drizzle of olive oil.

Basic risotto

Many people think that making a risotto is incredibly laborious and time-consuming, but generally speaking, it takes about 20 minutes from adding the first ladleful of stock.

You need to use short-grain risotto rice, such as Carnaroli or Arborio, and a vegetable- or chicken-based stock. I tend to avoid using fish stock, even for fish-based risotto, because I find it a little overpowering. The stock must be hot when you add it to the rice, as it needs to continue cooking the grains as soon as it hits the pan. Never add too much stock at any one time – a ladleful is fine. Most importantly, stir regularly. This will ensure a creamy risotto.

Make sure the butter added at the end is chilled when you stir it in (if the butter is warm, it just melts straight away and the risotto goes slushy rather than creamy). Once some grated Parmesan has been added, you should have a pourable, delicious risotto. This is the base for all the risotto recipes that follow.

Serves 4
2 tbsp olive oil
225 g cold butter, diced
1 small onion or 2 small shallots, chopped
350 g risotto rice
200 ml white wine
about 1.25 litres hot Vegetable stock (page 261)
100 g fresh Parmesan, finely grated
salt and freshly ground black pepper

Heat the oil and 25 g of the butter in a large pan over a medium heat. Add the onion and cook, stirring, until soft and translucent, about 2 minutes. Stir in the rice and cook for a further 2 minutes. Turn up the heat and add the wine – it should sizzle as it hits the pan. Cook for about 2 minutes to evaporate the alcohol.

Once the liquid has reduced, begin adding the hot stock a ladleful at a time over a medium heat, allowing each addition to be absorbed before adding the next, and stirring continuously. The rice should always be moist but not swimming in liquid. The process of adding and stirring should take about 16–18 minutes.

Remove from the heat and stir in the remaining butter. Finish with the Parmesan, then season well and serve.

Mushroom risotto

You make this with both fresh and dried mushrooms – soak the dried porcini and use the strained soaking juices as part of your stock. 'Porcini' is the Italian word for ceps, and they are usually labelled as such when you buy them dried.

Serves 4
50 g dried porcini mushrooms, covered with hot water and soaked for 5 minutes
100 g fresh ceps
4 tbsp olive oil
1 quantity Basic risotto (opposite)
salt and freshly ground black pepper

Drain the porcini, reserving the soaking liquid in a measuring jug.

Peel the stems of the ceps and wipe the caps with a damp cloth. Cut into slices and set aside.

Make the basic risotto, replacing the equivalent amount of vegetable stock with the mushroom liquid. Halfway through the cooking time, add the soaked porcini. Continue to the point where you remove the risotto from the heat.

Heat the olive oil in a pan over a high heat and add the ceps. Season and fry for 2–3 minutes, or until golden, turning. Remove and add to the risotto, along with the cold butter and Parmesan. Check the seasoning and serve.

Artichoke and langoustine risotto

Adding artichoke purée to a risotto is quite traditional, but we tarted it up for the Connaught by adding a decadent touch with the langoustines. You can substitute king prawns, or just leave them out altogether.

Serves 4
8 baby artichokes
80 ml olive oil
200 ml Vegetable stock (page 261)
3 garlic cloves, lightly crushed with the palm of your hand
2 sprigs of fresh thyme
1 bay leaf
12 raw langoustines or large king prawns, shelled
1 quantity Basic risotto (page 92), but using only 100 g butter
1 tbsp chopped fresh flatleaf parsley
salt and freshly ground black pepper

Cut the stems from the artichokes. Pull off the outer leaves and peel the area where the stalks were attached down to the flesh. Cut off the remaining leaves and scrape out all the hairy bits (the choke). Cut each heart into 4 pieces.

Heat 2 tablespoons of the olive oil in a medium pan. Add the artichoke hearts and some seasoning and cook, turning, until lightly coloured, about 3 minutes. Add a ladleful of the vegetable stock, along with 2 garlic cloves, 1 sprig of thyme and the bay leaf. Reduce the heat and cook for 5 minutes, adding more stock as it evaporates, until the artichokes are soft (the idea is to braise the artichokes).

Remove from the heat and discard the garlic and herbs. Put the artichokes and a little of the cooking juices in a blender or food processor and blitz into a smooth purée.

Make a shallow incision along the back of each langoustine or prawn, then use the tip of the knife to pull out the black intestinal tract. This should be discarded. Bring a pan of salted water to the boil and add the langoustines or prawns. Boil for 30–60 seconds to par-cook them. Drain and set aside.

Make the basic risotto up to the point of removing it from the heat. Stir in the artichoke purée, followed by 100 g butter and the parsley.

Meanwhile, heat the remaining 50 ml oil in a frying pan over a low heat. Add the blanched langoustines along with the remaining thyme and garlic. Cook for 1–2 minutes. Serve the langoustines on top of the finished risotto, drizzling over the juices from the pan.

Risotto quattro formaggio

Literally 'risotto with four cheeses', this is very rich indeed. You could replace any of the cheeses if you liked – perhaps try dolcelatte, pecorino or buffalo mozzarella instead.

Serves 4
1 quantity Basic risotto (page 92), but using only 25 g Parmesan and 100 g butter
25 g Gorgonzola, roughly chopped
25 g Fontina, roughly chopped
25 g Provolone, roughly chopped
1 tbsp chopped fresh flatleaf parsley
salt and freshly ground black pepper

Make the basic risotto to the point of removing it from the heat. Add all the cheeses together and allow to melt into the risotto. Finish by stirring in the butter and parsley. Check the seasoning and serve immediately.

Risotto with peas and broad beans

This risotto is the taste of summer – lovely fresh peas and broad beans in season.

Serves 4
200 g fresh peas, podded weight
200 g fresh broad beans, podded weight
½ quantity Basic risotto (page 92)
salt and freshly ground black pepper

Bring a pan of salted water to the boil and blanch the peas and beans in it for 2–3 minutes. Drain and set aside.

Make the basic risotto to the point of removing it from the heat. Add the peas and broad beans and season to taste. Stir in the butter and Parmesan and serve immediately.

Crab risotto

If you want to add even more richness to this already succulent risotto, you could whiz the herbs together in a mini-processor with some olive oil and drizzle over the top before serving.

Serves 2
2 tbsp brown crab meat
dash of Tabasco sauce
juice of ½ lemon
½ quantity Basic risotto (page 92),
using only 50 g butter and omitting
the Parmesan
125 g fresh white crab meat
handful of chopped fresh basil (chopped
at the last minute)
handful of chopped fresh flatleaf parsley
salt and freshly ground black pepper

Put the brown crab meat in a mini-processor with the Tabasco and lemon juice and blitz to combine. Check the seasoning.

Make the basic risotto up to the point of having added all the stock. Add the blitzed brown crab meat and cook for another 3 minutes. Remove from the heat and stir in the 50 g butter, together with the white crab meat, basil and parsley. Serve immediately.

Overleaf
Nonna (third from right)
with her parents (in the
centre of the photograph)
and all her brothers and
sisters (see the Family
Tree on pages 264–5)

Bomba di riso

My cousin Pino married a great cook, and this is one of Rina's best recipes. She always made fantastic bombas for scampagnatas – Italian parties that we had every summer in north London.
A bomba is essentially a stuffed rice cake that is set in a bowl. Rina traditionally filled it with pigeon ragù, but I've adapted it below to make a vegetarian version with mushrooms. It's an easy recipe, but you have to get the consistency right in order for the rice to stay in its bomba shape.

Serves 6–8
50 g butter, plus extra for greasing
100 g stale white breadcrumbs
1 quantity Basic risotto (page 92)
1 quantity Mushroom ragù (page 182)

Preheat the oven to 200°C/Gas Mark 6.

Butter a 20 cm Pyrex bowl and toss in a handful of the breadcrumbs. Tilt the bowl so that the crumbs coat the bottom and sides, then tip out the excess.

Taking about two-thirds of the risotto, use it to thickly line the base and sides of the bowl – the 'walls' of the bomba. Fill the centre with the mushroom ragù. Cover the top with the remaining rice and sprinkle with the remaining breadcrumbs. Dot the butter over the top.

Bake in the oven for about 20 minutes, until it is golden brown. Remove and allow to rest before running a sharp knife around the edge of the bowl, and turning out on a plate to serve.

Polenta

There are two forms of polenta – soft and firm. If you want the latter, simply make this basic recipe and allow it to set (see variation, below). If you're really pushed for time, you can use instant polenta, which will take half the time to cook. I prefer the traditional method used by Nonna – hard work but the results are infinitely more delicious.

Polenta is one of those foods that you either love or hate. My sister Anne never really liked it. Rather amusingly, she once appeared on the TV show Can't Cook, Won't Cook *(she didn't let on that she was my sister), and the meal she had to cook was polenta! Thankfully, she won, but I don't think she's ever made it again since.*

You can have polenta soft with meaty stews (it's pictured with the Veal stew on page 144), or leave it to set, then cut into slices and grill or fry it.

Serves 4–6
300 ml milk
1 tsp salt
300 g polenta flour
100 g butter
50 g freshly grated Parmesan

Put the milk in a large heavy-based pan with 1.2 litres water and the salt. Bring to the boil.

Meanwhile, fold a large piece of baking parchment in half, then open it out on a flat surface. Place the polenta flour on it and gather up the sides so that you form a sort of chute. This will enable you to pour the polenta flour into the water quickly in one even stream.

When the liquid is boiling, quickly pour in the polenta flour, whisking vigorously with a balloon whisk as you do so. Reduce the heat and simmer for 20 minutes, stirring constantly. The polenta should begin to come away from the sides of the pan when it is cooked.

Pour the polenta on to a wooden board and scatter over the butter and Parmesan. Allow to melt in. Serve with Veal stew (page 145) or Mushroom ragù (page 182).

Variation
Firm polenta: Make the polenta recipe, as above. Leave to cool. When cold slice into slabs with a sharp knife. You can reheat these pieces, either by frying in a knob of butter for a minute or two, or grilling with butter on top until golden brown. Serve with a few rashers of grilled bacon or pancetta, and freshly grated Parmesan scattered on top.

Potato gnocchi

People are afraid of making gnocchi, but I'm not sure why – perhaps because they can turn out stodgy, and because it does take a bit of trial and error to get them right. The trick is to keep the potatoes dry so that the gnocchi are fluffy and melt in the mouth: if you have to chew them, you've added too much egg or flour. You must also use the potato flesh while it is still hot – don't leave it to cool too much first. If you don't want to serve the gnocchi with tomato sauce, try them with Mushroom ragù (page 182).

Serves 6–8
6 large Maris Piper or King Edward potatoes (about 2 kg total weight)
100–200 g rock salt (enough to cover a roasting tin in a thick layer)
300–400 g plain or 'oo' flour (you'll have to judge how much to use as you're making the gnocchi)
pinch of freshly grated nutmeg
2 medium eggs, lightly beaten
1 quantity Basic tomato sauce (page 256)
handful of fresh basil leaves
salt and freshly ground black pepper
handful of freshly grated Parmesan, to serve

Preheat the oven to 200°C/Gas Mark 6.

Wash the potatoes well, pat dry with a cloth, then pierce all over with a fork. Scatter a thick layer of rock salt into a roasting tin, sit the potatoes on top and bake in the oven for 1½–2 hours, or until soft. Remove and allow to cool just enough to handle.

Cut the potatoes in half and scoop out the flesh. Sprinkle 300 g of the flour on to a work surface. Pass the potato flesh through a potato ricer or sieve, then add to the flour. Season well and sprinkle with the nutmeg. Make a well in the centre, pour in the eggs and gradually work in the flour and potato to form a soft dough. Take care not to overwork the mixture.

Bring a large pan of salted water to the boil. Take a teaspoon of the mixture and drop it into the boiling water to check that it holds together without breaking up. You may need to add a little more flour and test again.

When you're happy that the consistency is correct, cut the gnocchi dough into 6–8 pieces and roll into long sausage shapes about 2 cm in diameter. Cut each sausage into 3 cm lengths and roll each piece against the back of a fork.

Reduce the pan of water to a brisk simmer. To cook the gnocchi, drop in batches into the pan and cook for 2–2½ minutes, or until they rise to the surface. Using a slotted spoon, lift out and place in a warmed serving dish. (Note: You can par-cook the gnocchi in advance for use later: simply blanch in batches for 30 seconds, then remove and refresh in iced water. They can then be stored for up to 24 hours in the fridge on a lightly oiled plastic tray.)

Heat the tomato sauce and stir in the basil leaves. Pour the tomato sauce over the gnocchi and sprinkle with Parmesan before serving.

Seafood

My first proper encounter with fish was at my grandparents' fish and chip shop in Becontree, where I used to work for extra pocket money when I was about fifteen. Given that they came from a mountainous area of Italy where fresh fish isn't readily available, it's odd that they and their siblings chose to set up fish and chip shops. In Bardi any fish tends to be preserved, like *bacala* (salt cod), or simply frozen.

Bacala is a festive dish, traditionally prepared on Christmas Eve and served with a rich tomato sauce. I remember spending a wonderful Christmas in Italy in 1999 with the whole family, when my Auntie Silvia cooked an incredible dish of *bacala*. We ate it hungrily, and approval was unanimous – almost. Her husband Dorino famously announced: 'Non ho mangiato bene stasera.' ('I have not eaten well this evening.') That's a typical Italian man's response, as he would never acknowledge that his wife could cook as well as his mother. My brother Michael and I were greatly amused, and it's become his catchphrase after every meal. Luckily for him, we know he's joking!

Even the frozen fish in Italy is of fantastic quality, frozen the minute it's pulled out of the sea. My Uncle Piero makes a wonderful salad with frozen octopus. Also, Italian canned tuna is really good – more than acceptable in the Tuna, celery and haricot bean salad on page 181. But the fresh fish you get in Italy cannot be beaten. Down south in Puglia I found it was so fresh that it barely needed cooking – just searing over a wood barbecue for literally seconds on each side, then a squeeze of lemon juice. All along the Italian coast you find delicious shellfish, including langoustines, lobster, crabs and crayfish, and that classic clam dish, Spaghetti alle vongole (page 85). I fell in love with this dish as a teenager, while staying with my Auntie Maria and Piero in their little guest-house in Lignano, and I insisted on eating it every single day of the fortnight's holiday.

The fish dishes in this chapter are, I admit, mainly Connaught ones. They're actually very simple, and we make them just a bit more sophisticated for the hotel restaurant; for instance, we might wrap monkfish in Parma ham and serve with tapenade to take it to another level, but the recipe I've given is less complicated and just as delicious (page 120). Nonetheless, we still follow the basic rule, which is never to complicate fish. The more garnishes you add, the more you lose its essence and flavour.

Chargrilled king prawns with lime

In southern Italy succulent grilled prawns are the mainstay of local fish restaurants. These make great barbecue finger food, as you just peel off the shells and dip the prawns into a delicious aïoli or romesco sauce – so simple and flavoursome. Use fresh raw jumbo prawns if possible – frozen ones are all right at a pinch.

Serves 2 as a starter, but easy to adapt for more people
12 king or tiger prawns, with shell and head on
1–2 tbsp olive oil
grated zest and juice of 2 limes
salt and freshly ground black pepper
Aïoli or Romesco sauce, to serve (pages 42 and 258)

Place the prawns in a bowl with enough olive oil to coat lightly. Add the lime zest and juice and season well. Toss together and leave to marinate in the fridge for 5–10 minutes.

Preheat a griddle pan or barbecue until very hot. Cook the prawns for 2–3 minutes on each side, or until cooked through: this will depend on their size – make sure they're completely pink with no grey flesh remaining.

Remove from the heat and serve with your preferred dipping sauce.

Gratinated anchovies

You see fresh anchovies everywhere in Spain and Italy, but very rarely in the UK, so snap them up if your fishmonger has some. They are best served as part of an ensemble main course or among a selection of antipasti rather than as a main course in their own right. Serve from the baking dish with a crisp green salad dressed with Classic vinaigrette (page 262).

Serves 4
12–15 fresh anchovies, gutted
4–6 tbsp fresh white breadcrumbs
4 tbsp freshly grated Parmesan
2 tbsp finely chopped fresh mixed herbs, e.g. thyme, rosemary, parsley
½ garlic clove, crushed
juice and zest of ½ lemon or lime
salt and freshly ground black pepper

Preheat the grill to high.

Place the anchovies in a shallow ovenproof dish.

In a bowl mix together the breadcrumbs, Parmesan, herbs, garlic, lemon or lime juice and zest, and some seasoning. Sprinkle the herby mixture over the anchovies and grill for 3–4 minutes, until the topping is crisp and golden and the anchovies are cooked through.

Roast scallops with potatoes and pata negra

Scallops are always a favourite, and this particular dish is one we served at the Connaught a couple of summers ago. It's a delicious combination that includes pata negra (Spanish ham), though you could use good Parma ham instead. Don't even think about using frozen scallops – it just won't work. Get your fishmonger to take fresh scallops out of the shells for you.

Serves 4 as a starter
12–16 small new potatoes, cut in
half lengthways
50 ml olive oil
knob of butter
½ tsp mild curry powder
12 medium scallops, corals removed
8 slices pata negra or Parma ham, torn
into bite-sized pieces
½ quantity Classic vinaigrette
(page 262)
salt and freshly ground black pepper

Bring a pan of salted water to the boil. Cook the potatoes for 4–5 minutes to soften but not cook all the way through, then drain.

Heat the olive oil in a non-stick frying pan and add the potatoes. Reduce the heat and cook gently, stirring frequently, just to colour. Season, add the butter and let it bubble slightly without burning. Continue to turn the potatoes until cooked through – about 10–15 minutes. Remove from the pan and keep warm.

Mix ½ teaspoon of salt with the curry powder and use it to season the scallops.

Heat the frying pan over a high heat and gently place the scallops in it. Cook for 1–2 minutes, then turn and cook for another minute. (You have to be organized here: turn the scallops over in the order they went into the pan. This ensures they all cook for the same amount of time on each side.) The scallops should be a beautiful golden colour. Remove from the pan and drain on kitchen paper.

Divide the scallops and potatoes between four serving plates, scatter over a few pieces of pata negra and drizzle with the vinaigrette.

Stuffed sardines with orange dressing

I love sardines – such fantastic fish, and a real taste of the Mediterranean. We should be able to get fresh sardines all year round, but in the UK it's quite difficult. I do hope we start seeing them more often in fishmongers and restaurants. Roasting is by far the easiest way to cook sardines – stuff their insides, pop them in the oven and enjoy a delicious treat about 10 minutes later.

Serves 4
150 g stale white breadcrumbs
3 tbsp finely chopped fresh
flatleaf parsley
½ tsp chopped fresh thyme leaves
zest of 1 lemon, plus a squeeze of juice
3–4 tbsp olive oil, plus extra for
drizzling
8 sardines, scaled, gutted and cleaned
salt and freshly ground black pepper

For the orange dressing
250 ml olive oil
100 ml freshly squeezed orange juice
50 ml white wine vinegar

Preheat the oven to 190°C/Gas Mark 5.

Put the breadcrumbs, parsley, thyme and lemon zest and juice in a bowl, add some seasoning and stir. Pour in enough olive oil to bind the mixture and create a soft stuffing.

Stuff the mixture into the sardines and transfer to a lightly oiled ovenproof dish or roasting tin. Drizzle a little olive oil over the fish and add a splash of water to the tin: this will help to prevent the sardines drying out during cooking. Cover with foil and bake in the oven for 10–15 minutes.

Meanwhile, put the dressing ingredients in a bowl and whisk together. Add seasoning to taste.

Remove the sardines from the oven and serve immediately with the orange dressing drizzled over.

Fried soft-shelled crabs

Soft-shelled crabs are not just an American ingredient – they're quite common in southern Italy, where they're pan-fried. At the Connaught we use them in a lovely spaghetti dish, but here they're simply fried with olive oil and herbs. You can buy soft-shelled crabs frozen in packets in the UK – try Japanese shops, as they're often used in wraps and hand rolls. Serve this recipe very simply with a crisp green salad.

Serves 4
100 ml olive oil
3 garlic cloves, finely sliced
4 sprigs of fresh thyme
8–10 soft-shelled crabs
1 tbsp chopped fresh flatleaf parsley
salt

Heat the oil in a large frying pan over a high heat. Add the garlic and thyme and fry for 30 seconds, or until light golden. Add the crabs to the pan and cook until they turn bright red, about 4 minutes, turning them halfway through. Serve immediately, scattered with the parsley and sprinkled with salt.

Fritto misto

This is a very common dish along the Italian coast. Invariably, cooks will use squid or octopus in the mixture, but you can include anchovies, prawns or even bite-sized baby red mullet. Serve this wonderful dish of seafood simply with crushed rock salt and a squeeze of lemon juice – it's a taste of sunshine.

Serves 4

20 large raw tiger prawns, head and shell on
12 cleaned baby squid (chipirones)
150 g '00' flour, plus extra for dusting
250 ml ice-cold sparkling water
vegetable oil, for deep frying
salt and freshly ground black pepper

Remove the heads and shells from the prawns (you can use these for fish stock, if you like). Make a shallow incision along the back of each prawn, and use the tip of the knife to pull out the black intestinal tract. This should be discarded.

Wash the squid under cold running water, then pat dry with a cloth or kitchen paper.

Preheat a deep-fat fryer or a large pan of oil to 180°C.

Put the flour into a large bowl and place it over another bowl filled with iced water. (This helps to keep the batter mix cold, and therefore as light as possible.) Slowly pour in the sparkling water and mix with chopsticks. There's no need to beat the batter – lumps are fine.

Season the prawns and squid well and dust with a little flour. Dip each piece of fish individually into the batter and lower straight into the hot oil. Fry in batches for 5 minutes, or until crisp but not too dark.

Use a slotted or wire spoon to remove the fish from the oil, then drain on kitchen paper and keep warm. Repeat with the remaining fish, and serve immediately.

Grilled lobster

This is a fabulous, summery dish that I used to make when I was working in Barbados. Lobster's not my favourite shellfish as it can be chewy and quite tough, but this is a great way of cooking it: sear quickly on the grill pan, herb butter on top ... bang – done! You could also cook this in the oven, at 220°C/Gas Mark 7 for 6–8 minutes, until soft.

Serves 4

2 live lobsters, about 600–800 g each
100 g softened butter
2 garlic cloves, finely chopped
½ tbsp chopped fresh flatleaf parsley
½ tbsp chopped fresh tarragon
olive oil, for drizzling
salt and freshly ground black pepper

Place the lobsters in the freezer for a couple of hours while you tackle the first step. This will send them to sleep before you come to prepare them.

In a bowl mix together the butter, garlic and herbs. Season well and leave to set in the fridge. Once cold, dice into 5 mm cubes.

Take the lobsters out of the freezer. Position the point of a very sharp knife on the natural cross mark on the top of the head. Pressing down hard, bring down the knife to make a horizontal cut. Then make a vertical cut between the lobster's eyes. This kills the lobster instantly. Cut down through the back of the head and tail. Remove the dark vein running along the back of the tail. Discard the dirt sac from the head, as well as any green coral, so that you are left with just the tail and claw meat.

Drizzle a little olive oil on each lobster half and season. Heat a griddle pan until hot and place the lobster halves, cut side down, on it. Cook for 4–5 minutes, then turn over and place a few cubes of the herb butter on top. Finish grilling on the shell side for another 4–5 minutes. When cooked through, the lobster should be a bright red colour and the butter melted. Serve immediately.

Grilled swordfish

This dish has southern Italian origins, with the Moorish additions of capers and sultanas. Marinate the swordfish a little before grilling it to give it a nice, delicate flavour.

Serves 4
200 ml olive oil
juice of 1 lemon
50 g baby capers
100 g sultanas
4 x 150-g swordfish steaks,
about 2.5 cm thick
20 ml cider vinegar
2 tbsp finely chopped fresh
flatleaf parsley
salt and freshly ground black pepper

First, make a marinade by mixing together 100 ml of the olive oil with the lemon juice in a shallow dish. Stir in half the capers and sultanas. Add a little black pepper. Place the swordfish in the dish, coat well with the marinade and set aside for 30 minutes.

Preheat a griddle pan. Remove the swordfish from the marinade. Brush the griddle pan with olive oil and sear the swordfish for 2–3 minutes on each side. About halfway through the cooking time for each side, turn the fish by about 45 degrees so that you get a nice criss-cross pattern from the griddle.

Mix the remaining olive oil with the vinegar. Add the remaining capers and sultanas and stir in the parsley. Finish with freshly milled salt.

Transfer the swordfish to a plate and pour over the caper and sultana dressing before serving.

Red mullet with black olive vinaigrette

Red mullet is a very common fish in the Mediterranean: go to any restaurant along the Italian coast and chances are it will crop up on the menu. Mullet come in various sizes, ranging from tiny fish that you can use as part of Fritto misto (page 112) to larger specimens that can be roasted whole. I prefer to take large fish off the bone and pan-fry the fillets, as below.

Serves 4

8 x 220 g red mullet fillets, pin-boned
4 pinches of saffron
10 tbsp olive oil, plus extra for drizzling
1 large aubergine, peeled and cut into small dice
10 black olives, quartered
1 tbsp aged balsamic vinegar
salt and freshly ground black pepper

Place the red mullet on a baking sheet or in a roasting tin, skin-side up. Brush the fillets with 1 tablespoon of olive oil and sprinkle with the saffron. Cover with cling film and refrigerate for 2 hours.

Heat 2 tablespoons of the olive oil in a large frying pan over a low heat and add the aubergine. Cook for 10–15 minutes, until soft and cooked through.

Transfer the aubergine to a food processor and blend to a smooth purée. Season to taste and set aside, keeping warm.

To make the vinaigrette, mix the olives in a bowl with the balsamic vinegar and 6 tablespoons of olive oil. Blitz with a hand blender until most of the olives have broken down. At this point the vinaigrette will be quite thick: let it sit for 10 minutes and the vinegar and oil will separate, creating a split olive vinaigrette.

Season the red mullet. Heat the remaining 1 tablespoon of olive oil in a large frying pan over a high heat. Add the fish to the pan, skin-side down, and cook for 2 minutes, or until golden brown. Turn over and cook for a further 30 seconds.

Divide the aubergine purée between four serving plates. Top each mound with two red mullet fillets. Finish with a couple of tablespoons of the olive vinaigrette.

Roast monkfish with confit tomatoes

This is much more British than Italian, but excellent nonetheless. Monkfish can often be bland and needs a bit of a kick. It's also quite watery, so at the Connaught we roast it in a pan, throw in some confit (semi-dried) tomatoes right at the end, and deglaze it with a little balsamic vinegar to give a rich, potent flavour. You could try this with any white fish if you prefer not to use monkfish.

Serves 4

4 x 150 g pieces of monkfish tail,
grey membrane removed
200 ml olive oil, plus 2 tbsp
8 baby or small fennel bulbs
3 tbsp balsamic vinegar
small handful of fresh basil leaves
salt and freshly ground black pepper

For the confit tomatoes
4 plum tomatoes, skinned,
seeded and halved
1 tbsp olive oil
2 tsp fine rock salt
½ tsp freshly ground black pepper
2 tsp caster sugar
2 tsp fresh thyme leaves

Preheat the oven to 100°C/Gas Mark ¼.

Start by making the confit tomatoes. Put the tomato halves cut-side down on a baking sheet and sprinkle over the oil, salt, pepper, sugar and thyme leaves. Bake in the oven for about 3 hours, or until they are dried and shrivelled. Remove and set aside.

Increase the oven temperature to 180°C/Gas Mark 4.

Season the monkfish. Heat the 200 ml olive oil in a non-stick, ovenproof frying pan over a high heat, add the fish and cook for 5–6 minutes, turning halfway through, until golden. Remove from the heat and put directly into the oven. Bake for 5 minutes, then remove and set aside to rest for another 5 minutes.

Meanwhile, heat 2 tablespoons of olive oil in a large pan, add the fennel and season well. Cook, turning occasionally, for 5 minutes or until golden all over. Lower the heat and add the confit tomatoes, as well as the rested monkfish. Gently roll all the ingredients together in the pan juices, then add the balsamic vinegar. Allow it to bubble and reduce, scraping the base of the pan with a wooden spoon. Add the basil, then check the seasoning and adjust if necessary.

Slice each monkfish portion in half before serving with the confit tomatoes and fennel, and the pan juices poured over.

Halibut with pepper confit and fennel salad

I first tried this dish in California, and liked it so much that I put it on the menu at the Connaught. The fish is not at all greasy, despite being cooked in a lot of olive oil; it's simply moist and white. (This cooking method can also be used for hake and sea bass.) You can either buy the halibut ready-portioned from your fishmonger, or get a small whole fish and freeze the portions that you don't use.

Serves 4

2 red peppers
2 yellow peppers
400 ml olive oil
6 sprigs of fresh thyme
2 sprigs of fresh rosemary
4 garlic cloves, lightly crushed with the palm of your hand
1 fennel bulb
4 x 150 g skinless halibut portions
1 tsp finely chopped fresh basil (chopped at the last minute)
dash of Classic vinaigrette (page 262)
1 tbsp finely chopped fresh dill
salt and freshly ground black pepper

Preheat the oven to 200°C/Gas Mark 6.

Put the peppers in a roasting tin and pour over 100 ml of the olive oil, rubbing it all over the skins of the peppers. Toss in 3 sprigs of the thyme, the rosemary, 2 garlic cloves and a pinch of salt. Roast for 10–15 minutes, turning halfway through, until the skin of the peppers starts to blacken and blister.

Remove from the oven, place the peppers in a bowl and cover tightly with cling film. This allows the peppers to steam, which loosens the skin. While they are still semi-hot, peel off the skin, discard the stalk and seeds, and cut the flesh into strips. Try to reserve the lovely sweet juices that come out while you're doing this. You can store the peppers in their juices in the refrigerator for up to two days.

Slice the fennel very finely by hand or on a mandoline. Transfer to a bowl of iced water until ready to use (this will stop the fennel going brown and keeps it nice and crisp).

Put the remaining 300 ml of olive oil into a frying pan just large enough to hold all the halibut in one layer. Heat the oil to 54°C (you'll need to use a thermometer for this). Add some seasoning and the remaining 3 sprigs of thyme and 2 garlic cloves. Add the fish and cook gently at a constant temperature of 54°C for 15 minutes, turning halfway through, until the fish is evenly cooked.

Meanwhile, gently reheat the peppers in a pan. Remove from the heat and stir in the basil. Check the seasoning.

Drain the fennel and pat dry with a tea towel. Mix with a dash of the vinaigrette (enough to taste, but not so much that you drown the fennel) and half of the chopped dill.

Remove the halibut from the oil and drain on kitchen paper.

To serve, spoon the peppers on to individual plates. Place a piece of halibut on top, followed by the remaining dill. Finish with a handful of the fennel salad on top.

Baked baby sea bass

This is the ideal dish if you're having people over for dinner, as there's absolutely no messing around – just stuff the fish with herbs and lemon, stick it in the oven and it's done. Use sea bream if you can't get hold of whole bass (see the photo opposite, where I've cooked both).

Serves 4
olive oil, for greasing
2 baby sea bass, about 600–800 g each,
gutted, cleaned and descaled, with
eyes removed
½ bunch fresh dill
½ bunch fresh flatleaf parsley
1 lemon, sliced
1 celery stick, cut into 6
½ fennel bulb, cut into strips
1 whole head of garlic, sliced horizontally
4 sprigs of fresh thyme
250 ml white wine
salt and freshly ground black pepper
400 g new potatoes, to serve

Preheat the oven to 200°C/Gas Mark 6.

Lightly grease the base of a large, deep roasting tin or dish with olive oil; the tin should be large enough to hold the fish flat. Place the sea bass side by side in the tin.

Stuff half the herbs into the fish, along with half the lemon slices.

Scatter the remaining herbs and lemon slices over the top of the fish, add the celery, fennel, garlic and thyme to the dish and season. Pour the wine around the fish, then cover tightly with foil and bake for 15 minutes, basting with the cooking juices halfway through. The fish is cooked when the flesh flakes easily with a fork or knife.

Meanwhile, bring the new potatoes to the boil in a pan of salted water. Reduce the heat and simmer until tender. Remove from the heat and drain.

Remove the fish from the oven, place on a large plate and serve immediately with the boiled potatoes.

Cod with chicory

When I worked in my grandparents' fish and chip shop as a schoolgirl, cod was always the most popular fish. Of course, times have changed, and cod is now under threat from overfishing. You could easily make this dish with pollack or John Dory instead. Adding sugar to the chicory caramelizes it, and the lovely sweet and sour flavours set off the plainness of the fish.

Serves 4
½ tsp icing sugar
6 baby chicory, cut in half lengthways
6 tbsp olive oil
4 x 150 g cod fillets, skin on
salt and freshly ground black pepper

Place the icing sugar in a bowl and add the chicory halves. Toss until fully coated.

Heat a griddle pan until hot. Drizzle over 3 tablespoons of the olive oil. Put the chicory cut-side down on the grill pan and place a heavy pan or plate on top; this keeps the chicory firmly in contact with the griddle and allows it to caramelize. Cook for 3–4 minutes on the cut side, then turn over, season and weight down again for 2–3 minutes. Remove from the heat and keep warm.

Season the cod with salt and pepper. Heat the remaining 3 tablespoons of olive oil in a non-stick frying pan and cook the seasoned cod in it, skin-side down, for 3–4 minutes, until the skin is browned and crisp. Turn carefully (cod breaks very easily) and cook on the other side for 3–4 minutes, or until the flesh is just cooked and opaque.

Put three pieces of chicory on each serving plate and top with the cooked cod. Spoon over the juices from the frying pan before serving.

Hake with romesco crust

I tasted this combination of flavours in Spain when I was travelling around the Mediterranean for a few months exploring restaurants and recipes. I love the piquant peppers with the almonds and garlic, spicy and savoury at the same time. It works really well with most fish, including cod and halibut, but hake is the Spanish favourite.

Serves 4

1 x 290 g jar roasted red peppers, drained and cut into quarters
1 tbsp fresh rosemary leaves, chopped
2 garlic cloves, sliced
3 tbsp olive oil
50 g skinned salted almonds
50 g dry white breadcrumbs
2 medium courgettes
4 x 150 g hake portions, skin on
salt and freshly ground black pepper

Preheat the oven to 100°C/Gas Mark ¼.

Lay the peppers on a baking sheet. Sprinkle over the rosemary, garlic, 1 tablespoon of olive oil and some seasoning. Place in the oven and bake for 2 hours to dry out the peppers. Remove from the oven and allow to cool. Increase the oven temperature to 180°C/Gas Mark 4.

Once cool, place the peppers in a food processor with the almonds and breadcrumbs and blend until they have a sandy texture.

Slice the courgettes into discs 5 mm thick. Heat 1 tablespoon of olive oil in a non-stick frying pan, add the courgettes and season. Cook for 2–3 minutes on each side or until golden. Remove from the pan and set aside.

Heat the remaining 1 tablespoon of olive oil in the frying pan over a high heat. Add the hake portions, skin-side down, and cook for 2 minutes, or until the skin is golden brown. Transfer to a baking sheet, skin-side up, and sprinkle the prepared topping over the fish. Bake in the oven for 5–7 minutes, or until the flesh offers no resistance when you pierce it with the tip of a knife. Place the courgettes on individual plates and top with a piece of hake. Finish by spooning over some of the cooking juices.

Meat

Emilia-Romagna has, arguably, the best cuisine in Italy, but it certainly isn't the lightest. Most meals revolve around meat: you might start with prosciutto, follow this with tagliatelle with ragù, and then go on to braised veal. Even for the most enthusiastic carnivore, that's a lot of flesh. But it's all about balance: Italians don't have additional carbohydrates such as potatoes with the meat main course, just salad or vegetables.

The quality of Italian meat is excellent. On a recent trip to Tuscany with four other chefs, we were invited to a wine supplier's home for some traditional food. One of the courses was *carni crude* – diced-up raw veal. Everyone looked to me (with slightly worried expressions) for advice. I explained that you put it on toast, season it well, add a touch of local olive oil, and it's the best thing you've ever eaten in your life. After tasting it, they couldn't help but agree. Of course, you can only do this with top-quality meat, which is cut up by hand so there is absolutely no sinew or fat.

The history of meat dishes in Emilia-Romagna stems very much from peasant eating habits. One large piece of meat, such as braised beef, would be stretched out for several more meals, either eaten on its own, or as part of Anolini (page 76), or eaten cold with mustard fruits. Slow cooking was key:

a rich stew, such as Osso bucco (page 157), would go on the stove in the morning and be cooked to melting tenderness by the evening.

Nonna never skimped on quality, and always bought the best meat she could. She even picked up the very English tradition of the Sunday roast, and absolutely loved Yorkshire pudding. I used to go with her and Mum to an amazing butcher's shop in Upminster – I loved those visits, hearing what Nonna asked for and watching the butcher cut up the meat. It seems such a shame that butchering is a dying tradition in the UK these days, and that as a nation of farmers we have so few dedicated shops left to prepare and sell our wonderful livestock. If you have a local butcher's, do support it.

In this chapter I've included lots of classic Italian family dishes, plus a few more 'sophisticated' ones that we might serve at the Connaught, including Roast pigeon with sausage and date stuffing (page 138) and Lamb rack niçoise (page 152).

P.S. I must confess that I once decided to give up meat for Lent. My sacrifice lasted all of two days. When I went to Nonna's house for supper and she had made Cotoletta (page 140), there was no way I could resist, and my stint at being a vegetarian came to a very abrupt end.

Roast chicken with lemon, thyme and garlic

It's hard to go wrong with roast chicken, though some people manage it. The fundamental rule is always to use a good chicken – corn-fed, plus free-range or organic. Never, ever use a frozen chicken – you only have to defrost one to see how much water comes out of it; there's very little actual meat there. I like to wrap the bird in foil to steam and roast it at the same time – pop a bit of stock in the roasting tin to keep the flesh really moist. This version of roast chicken is traditionally Italian, being cooked with lots of garlic, thyme, tarragon and lemon. I like it served with a simple green salad, but you can do all the Sunday lunch trimmings if you like.

Serves 6–8

2 corn-fed, organic or free-range chickens, approx. 1–1.2 kg each
50 g butter, softened
drizzle of olive oil
1 small bunch of fresh thyme
2 tbsp chopped tarragon leaves
1 head of garlic, cloves separated but unpeeled and lightly crushed with the palm of your hand
1 lemon, sliced
150 ml Chicken stock (page 260)
salt and freshly ground black pepper

Preheat the oven to 200°C/Gas Mark 6.

Line a large ovenproof dish or roasting tin with two large pieces of foil – big enough to wrap around the chickens with room to spare.

Place the chickens on the foil inside the dish and rub them all over with the butter and olive oil. Season well and place half the thyme, tarragon, garlic and lemon inside the cavities, scattering the remainder over and around the chickens.

Pour in the stock, then wrap the foil loosely around the chickens to seal while still allowing air to circulate.

Place in the oven for 1 hour 20 minutes, then turn down the heat to 180°C/Gas Mark 4 and cook for a further 15 minutes. About 10 minutes before the end of the cooking time, open up the foil to allow the chicken to colour.

To test whether the chicken is cooked, stick the tip of a knife into the thickest part of the thigh; if the juices run clear, it's ready. If the juices are still pink, give the birds another 10–15 minutes.

Remove from the oven and transfer to a plate or tin to rest for 10–15 minutes before carving.

Chicken cacciatore

The classic dish of 'hunter's chicken' doesn't use the white meat of the bird, so it's very economical – the Italian version of pot roast. I really like this cold. You can take the lovely braised legs or thighs to nibble on as part of a picnic lunch.

Serves 4
2 tbsp olive oil
knob of butter
4 chicken legs, cut in half to separate thighs and drumsticks
2 heads of garlic, cut in half horizontally
small bunch of fresh rosemary
½ glass white wine
300–350 ml Chicken stock (page 260)
salt and freshly ground black pepper

Heat the olive oil and butter in a heavy-based pan or casserole over a medium heat.

Season the chicken pieces and add to the pan along with the garlic and rosemary. Cook until the chicken has browned evenly – about 8 minutes – turning halfway through.

Turn up the heat and pour in the white wine, letting it bubble until it reduces. When most of the wine has evaporated, add enough stock to half-cover the chicken pieces. Reduce the heat and cover with a lid or a cartouche (a circle of baking parchment). Simmer for 25–30 minutes, basting the chicken occasionally to ensure it stays moist.

Spoon off any excess fat that has risen to the surface during cooking, and serve the chicken with the tasty juices.

Roast duck with mustard fruits

This is a traditional roast duck, but I've added my own Italian twist by serving it with preserved mustard fruits, which cut beautifully through the fattiness of the duck. I prefer the flavour of Moulard ducks, but Gressingham ducks are fine for this recipe, and you can use just duck breasts if you don't want to go to the trouble of roasting a whole bird.

Serves 3–4
1 duck, approx. 1–1.2 kg
1 quantity Mustard fruits (page 250)
salt and freshly ground black pepper

Preheat the oven to 220°C/Gas Mark 7.

Trim any excess fat from the duck, especially around the cavity and at the neck end. Using a sharp knife, score the skin all over so that the fat will render down more easily. Season well inside and out, then place on a trivet in a roasting tin. Roast in the oven for 45 minutes to 1 hour, or until the skin is crisp and the juices running from the cavity are clear.

Remove and allow to rest for at least 10 minutes before carving. Serve with the mustard fruits.

Chargrilled quail

This is a perfect barbecue dish. If you like, you can ask your butcher to de-bone and flatten out the quails for you. Once that's done, the dish couldn't be simpler: marinate for an hour or two, then put the birds straight on the grill. The marinating and the high heat stop the meat drying out. Use pigeons or poussins if you can't get hold of quails. Serve with a green salad.

Serves 4
4 quails
3 tbsp olive oil
½ lemon, thinly sliced
1 red onion, thinly sliced
1 garlic clove, thinly sliced
2 sprigs of fresh rosemary
salt and freshly ground black pepper

Put each bird breast-side up on a board and use a very sharp knife or poultry shears to cut down the middle, from end to end, along each side of the backbone. Work your way down the bones, gently easing the breast flesh away from the carcass. When you reach the joints for the legs and wings, break them; the bones should pop out of the sockets fairly easily. Once you have pulled all the meat away from the main breastbone, you should be able to remove the backbone, ribcage and breastbone in one piece. Bone out the thigh by scraping around the bone until it comes loose. Leave the leg bones in.

Place the boned quails in a bowl or roasting tin and drizzle with the olive oil. Add the lemon, onion, garlic and rosemary and mix everything together. Leave to marinate for at least 30 minutes, but no more than 1½ hours.

When you are ready to cook the quails, heat a griddle pan until very hot. Remove the birds from the marinade along with a few bits of onion and lemon, season and grill for 5 minutes on each side until golden.

Roast pigeon with sausage and date stuffing

The spicy flavours here are inspired by the dishes of southern Italy, where there's a strong Moorish influence in the ingredients and seasonings. You could serve this with mashed potatoes or roasted parsnips, or even just a green salad as it's quite rich.

Serves 4
6 small Cumberland sausages
2 knobs of butter
1 large onion, chopped
10 dried dates, stoned and halved
50 g flaked almonds, lightly toasted in a dry frying pan
4 pigeons
2 tbsp olive oil
8 rashers streaky bacon
salt and freshly ground black pepper

Preheat the oven to 180°C/Gas Mark 4.

Split the sausages, discard the skins and put the meat in a bowl. Set aside.

Heat a knob of the butter in a pan over a medium heat. Add the onion and cook until soft and golden brown, about 5 minutes. Remove and add to the sausage meat, along with the dates and almonds. Season well. Loosely stuff each pigeon with the sausage mixture and season the outsides.

Heat the olive oil with the remaining knob of butter in a large frying pan until foaming. Add the pigeons and colour on all sides, turning occasionally, about 5 minutes. Remove from the pan and place on a baking sheet or in a roasting tin or ovenproof dish, breast-side up. Cover each pigeon breast with two rashers of bacon – this will help to prevent the meat drying out during cooking. Roast in the oven for 10–12 minutes.

Cotoletta of veal

I love this dish – fine pieces of veal coated in crisp breadcrumbs. Although it's pretty straightforward, you must take care to get the pieces nicely coated and not overcooked inside or out. Serve it very simply, with lemon.

Serves 4
200 g plain flour
4 eggs, beaten
200 g stale white breadcrumbs
4 x 150–200 g veal escalopes (ask your butcher to beat them flat for you)
4 tbsp olive oil, plus extra for drizzling
knob of butter
2 tbsp chopped fresh parsley
2 tbsp capers, rinsed and finely chopped
1 lemon, cut into quarters
salt and freshly ground black pepper

Put the flour, eggs and breadcrumbs into three separate dishes and season each one.

Using tongs or a fork (fingers get very messy), take a veal escalope and place it in the flour, turning it so that both sides are well dusted. Shake off any excess, then dip it into the egg mixture. Again, shake off the excess and then place the veal in the breadcrumbs, making sure both sides are evenly coated. Set aside on baking parchment until ready to cook. Repeat with the remaining escalopes. Don't leave the veal sitting around for too long or the breadcrumbs will become soggy and won't crisp up when fried.

Heat 2 tablespoons of the oil and the butter in a large frying pan over a medium heat until bubbling. Carefully place the veal escalopes in the pan and fry gently for 3–4 minutes on each side, or until golden brown and nicely crisp. Remove from the pan and drain on kitchen paper.

Drain off all the oil from the pan and heat the remaining 2 tablespoons of olive oil in it over a high heat. Add the parsley and capers, toss well, and pour over the cotolettas. Drizzle over a little olive oil, if liked, and serve immediately, with the lemon quarters for squeezing over.

Veal chops with sage and Parma ham

This is my interpretation of the classic Italian saltimbocca*. It's quite a hearty dish, and should be served simply with a few sautéed mushrooms. If you really want to be decadent, or just plain greedy, you could serve it with buttery mashed potato. When you buy the chops, ask the butcher to scrape the bones clean for you. They should already be relatively clean, but it's nice to have them spotless for aesthetic purposes.*

Serves 4

4 x 400–500 g veal chops
8 fresh sage leaves
8 slices Parma ham
4 tbsp olive oil
100 g fresh ceps, wiped clean with a damp cloth and sliced
100 g fresh morels, wiped clean with a damp cloth and sliced
50 g butter
2 tbsp chopped fresh parsley
salt and freshly ground black pepper

Preheat the oven to 180°C/Gas Mark 4.

Season the chops on both sides. Place 1 sage leaf on each side of the chops, then wrap 2 slices of Parma ham around each one.

Heat 2 tablespoons of olive oil in an ovenproof frying pan. Add the chops and cook to brown the ham.

Transfer to the oven and roast for 15–20 minutes, turning the chops halfway through. Remove and set aside to rest for 5 minutes.

Meanwhile, heat the remaining 2 tablespoons of olive oil in a frying pan over a medium heat. Add the ceps, season, and cook for 1 minute. Add the morels and cook for another 1–2 minutes or until golden. Add the butter and allow to melt in. Check the seasoning and stir in the parsley. Remove from the heat.

Carve the veal chops and place on individual plates or boards with the mushrooms, drizzling over the cooking juices before serving.

Veal stew

My grandmother used to make fantastic stews with beef and veal, and I learnt from her that they're much better made in advance and allowed to rest so that the flavours have a chance to develop. This stew goes well with soft polenta (page 101).

Serves 4

2 tbsp olive oil

1 kg veal, cut into 2.5 cm cubes

1 onion, chopped

2 garlic cloves, chopped

4 carrots, sliced at an angle

2 sprigs of fresh thyme

1 tbsp tomato purée

350–400 ml Chicken stock (page 260) or water

handful of fresh flatleaf parsley leaves, finely sliced at the last minute, to serve

Preheat the oven to 180°C/Gas Mark 4.

Heat the olive oil in a heavy-based casserole. Add the veal and cook for 5–8 minutes without stirring or moving the meat, until it is coloured on one side – then turn it and brown on the other side. You want it to caramelize rather than boil in its own juices.

Remove the veal from the pan, drain in a sieve or colander, and set aside.

Place the onion and garlic in the pan and lightly sauté for 2–3 minutes. Add the carrots and thyme, and continue to cook until golden brown.

Return the veal to the pan and add the tomato purée. Stir well and cook for a further 2 minutes. Add enough stock or water to cover, bring to a simmer, then cover with a cartouche (a circle of baking parchment). Transfer to the oven for 1–1½ hours, stirring every 30 minutes and topping up with a little water if it's drying out. After 1½ hours, if the sauce seems a bit thin, cook for another 10–15 minutes. The veal is done when it is soft and melting enough to cut with a spoon. At this stage you can leave the stew to rest and then re heat when you want to eat it. Scatter over the parsley and serve.

Saltimbocca

Meaning literally 'jump into the mouth', saltimbocca consists of thin slices of veal fillet, wrapped around Parma ham, that are skewered and then slowly roasted. This recipe can also be made with beef fillet. When I was a little girl, I thought it was the height of sophistication because it was a snack with a toothpick through it!

Serves 4

12 slices veal topside, each about 1 cm thick
12 small fresh sage leaves
12 slices Parma ham
plain flour, for dusting
50 g butter
100 ml olive oil
150 ml dry white wine
salt and freshly ground black pepper

Place the slices of veal between two pieces of cling film. Pound with a rolling pin or the flat side of a meat cleaver until thin and completely flattened. Season well. Place one sage leaf on each slice, followed by a slice of Parma ham. Roll up, secure with a wooden toothpick and dust lightly with flour.

Heat the butter and olive oil in a frying pan over a high heat. Add the veal rolls and cook, turning, for 3–4 minutes, or until golden brown. Add the white wine and allow to bubble until completely reduced. Add a splash of water to moisten and cook for about 5 minutes. Remove the toothpicks and serve immediately.

Opposite
Me, looking suspiciously angelic, aged 3, in our garden at home in Densole, Kent

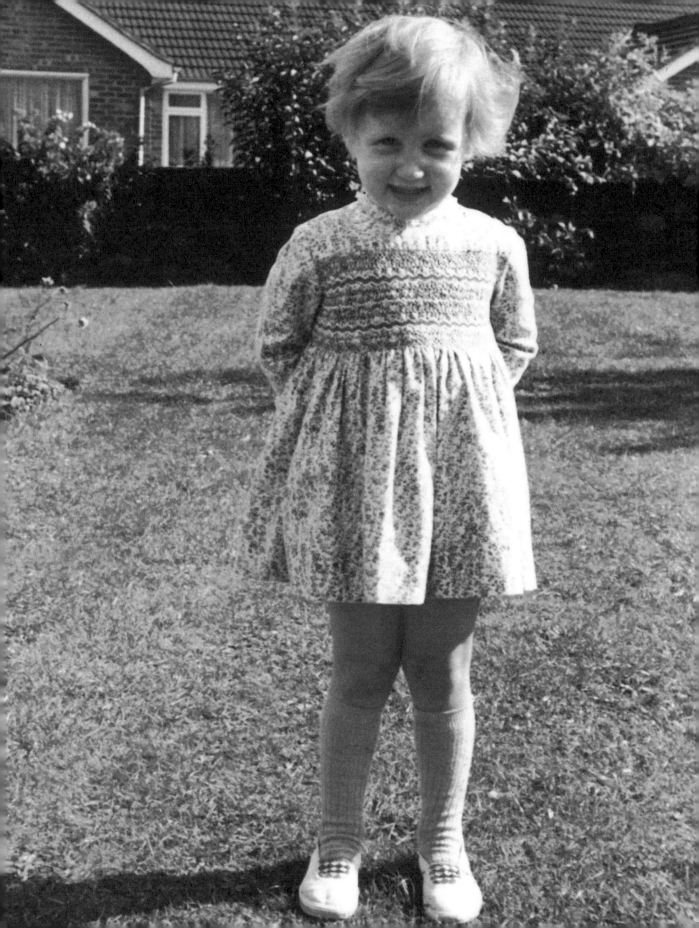

Stuffed rabbit legs

Rabbit meat is very common in Emilia-Romagna because rabbits are found in such abundance there, but it's still not popular in Britain. I think that too many people have had bland, farmed rabbit, which can be sadly lacking in flavour; use wild rabbit if you can find it. In this recipe the legs are boned, then filled with a tasty mixture of potato, pancetta and sage, and roasted. They go well with a soft polenta that doesn't overwhelm the delicate flavour of the meat (page 101).

Serves 4
4 rabbit legs
50 ml olive oil, plus a little extra
1 large Maris Piper potato, peeled and cut into 5 mm cubes
100 g pancetta, cut into 5 mm cubes
1 leek, finely sliced
2 tsp chopped fresh sage
2 tsp chopped fresh parsley
100–150 g butter
1 whole head of garlic, sliced in half horizontally
leaves from 2 sprigs of fresh thyme, chopped
2 sprigs of fresh rosemary
salt and freshly ground black pepper.

Carefully remove the thigh bone from each rabbit leg by making a straight incision along the leg, then cutting and scraping around the bone without breaking any of the meat. Set aside.

Heat the olive oil in a frying pan and add the potato. Fry for 5 minutes, or until half-cooked and golden. Add the pancetta to the pan and cook for 3–4 minutes, or until nicely browned. Add the leek and continue to cook for 3 minutes, or until the leek is soft. Remove from the heat and leave to cool.

When the mixture has cooled, add the sage and parsley, and season to taste. Stuff the mixture inside the rabbit legs and tie them up into neat parcels with kitchen string so that they retain their shape: no stuffing should be spilling out. Season the legs.

Preheat the oven to 180°C /Gas Mark 4.

Heat a drizzle of olive oil in a large, ovenproof frying pan over a medium heat. Add a knob of the butter and heat until foaming. Place the rabbit and garlic in the pan and cook for 5–10 minutes, browning the meat lightly on all sides. Add the remaining butter, and the thyme and rosemary, and shake the pan to coat the rabbit in the herby, buttery juices. Place the pan in the oven and cook for 8–10 minutes. Remove and serve on individual plates.

Roast leg of lamb

Lamb goes so well with garlic and rosemary that there's no point in complicating matters by adding other powerful flavours. Cooking the lamb on the bone helps the joint to retain its natural shape, but if you like, you can ask your butcher to bone it to make carving easier. This simple roast is great served with either Peperonata or Aubergine parmigiana (pages 172 and 178).

Serves 4
1 leg of lamb, approx. 1.35–2.25 kg
2 whole heads of garlic, cut in half horizontally, plus 8 cloves, sliced
5 sprigs of fresh rosemary
8 carrots, peeled and cut in half lengthways
2–4 tbsp olive oil
salt and freshly ground black pepper

Preheat the oven to 220°C/Gas Mark 7.

Make slits all over the lamb with the point of a sharp knife. Place a few slices of garlic and a few rosemary needles in each slit. Season the lamb all over.

Pour the olive oil into a large roasting tin. Add the garlic bulbs, remaining rosemary and carrots and toss to coat in the oil. Sit the lamb in the tin. Roast in the oven for 15 minutes, then turn the heat down to 180°C/Gas Mark 4 and cook for a further 45 minutes to 1 hour (basically it's 20 minutes per 450 g, plus another 20 minutes, but it depends on how pink you like your meat).

Remove the lamb from the oven, transfer to a plate or draining tray, reserving the juices, and allow to rest for 10–15 minutes. Spoon any excess fat from the roasting tin and discard, then stir in any juices from the resting lamb. Carve the lamb and serve with the carrots and the juices poured over.

Lamb rack niçoise

Here's an elegant dish that is easier to make than it appears. Ask your butcher to chine (remove the backbone) and French-trim the lamb racks for you so that the finished dish is easy to carve. You can make a large quantity of the breadcrumb crust and keep it in the freezer to use as and when needed – it doesn't have to be fresh every time. For the best result, use good-quality Provençal olives in oil.

Serves 4

generous handful of fresh flatleaf parsley leaves
1 tsp chopped fresh rosemary leaves
1 tsp chopped fresh thyme leaves
2 garlic cloves, roughly chopped
250 g white breadcrumbs, half dry and half fresh
2 French-trimmed racks of lamb
50 g butter
2 tbsp olive oil
50 g Dijon mustard
salt and freshly ground black pepper

For the niçoise garnish

3 tbsp olive oil, plus extra for drizzling
1 large courgette, cut into 5 mm dice
4 small bunches of vine-ripened cherry tomatoes
1 tbsp sugar
1 tbsp balsamic vinegar
10 black olives, pitted
handful of fresh basil leaves

Put the parsley in a food processor and blitz until finely chopped. Add the rosemary, thyme and garlic and blitz again. Add the breadcrumbs a handful at a time until you are left with a fine, vivid green mixture.

Preheat the oven to 240°C/Gas Mark 9.

Season the lamb all over. Heat the butter and oil in a large frying pan or roasting tin until hot and foaming. Add the lamb racks and cook, turning, for about 5 minutes, or until browned on all sides. Place in the hot oven for 4 minutes, then remove and leave to rest for at least 10 minutes.

Meanwhile, prepare the niçoise garnish. Heat 2 tablespoons of olive oil in a small frying pan over a medium heat and cook the courgette for 2–3 minutes, or until softened. Remove from the heat and set aside.

Place the cherry tomatoes, still on the vine, in a baking tray and drizzle with the remaining tablespoon of olive oil. Season and drizzle over the sugar and vinegar. Roast for 5 minutes, or until the tomato skins start to blister. Remove and set aside, keeping warm.

Brush the lamb with the mustard, then roll it in the breadcrumb mixture to coat all over. Return to the oven for 5 minutes.

Mix the courgette, olives and basil in a bowl and season. Remove the lamb from the oven and rest it briefly before cutting into slices. Place 2–3 cutlets on each plate, together with a bunch of tomatoes. Spoon the courgette mixture around the lamb and finish with a drizzle of olive oil.

Meatballs in tomato sauce

The secret of making light meatballs is to add bread and milk: these bind the mixture together, and also give it a lovely softness. If you want to spice things up a bit, add a touch of Tabasco or chopped garlic. They're good served with a few lightly sautéed new potatoes.

Serves 4
6 tbsp milk
1 thick slice of stale white bread,
crusts removed
500 g good-quality minced beef
1 small onion, finely chopped
1 tbsp finely chopped fresh
flatleaf parsley
4 tbsp freshly grated Parmesan
1 egg, beaten
flour, for dusting
200 ml olive oil, for frying
1 quantity Basic tomato sauce
(page 256)
2 tbsp chopped fresh parsley
salt and freshly ground black pepper

For the sautéed potatoes
400 g new potatoes
4 tbsp olive oil
1 garlic clove, lightly crushed with the
palm of your hand
1 sprig of fresh rosemary

Put the milk in a bowl, soak the bread in it, then mash together with a fork.

In another bowl mix together the beef, onion, parsley and Parmesan. Season well.

Add the bread mixture to the beef, then mix in the beaten egg. Before you make the meatballs, check that the seasoning is right by frying and tasting a teaspoon of the mixture; adjust the seasoning as necessary.

With floured hands, roll pieces of the mixture into balls about 5 cm in diameter. Set aside.

In a wide, shallow pan large enough to hold all the meatballs in one layer, heat the olive oil over a medium heat. Add the meatballs and cook until browned all over, turning very gently to prevent them breaking up. Remove from the pan and drain off the excess oil.

Return the meatballs to the pan and pour in the tomato sauce. Cover with baking parchment or foil, and cook gently over a low heat for 25 minutes.

Meanwhile, prepare the potatoes. Place the potatoes in a pan of salted water and bring to the boil. Boil for 10 minutes, then drain. Cut in half while still warm. Heat the oil in a frying pan over a medium heat, add the potatoes, garlic and rosemary, and cook for 4–5 minutes until the potatoes are tender and golden. Remove from the heat and discard the garlic and rosemary.

Remove the meatballs from the heat, sprinkle with the parsley and serve immediately, along with the potatoes. The meatballs can be stored in the refrigerator for up to 2 days.

Rib-eye beef with tomatoes and olives

In the UK we don't tend to associate olives with beef, but they give it a fantastic saltiness. This recipe is like an Italian version of classic British steak with roast tomatoes. You don't have to use rib-eye steak; thin slices of rump or fillet will do just as well.

Serves 4
1 tbsp butter
2 tbsp olive oil
4 x 200 g rib-eye steaks
4 plum tomatoes, seeded and quartered
10 black olives, pitted and coarsely chopped
10 caperberries, cut in half
1 quantity Red wine vinaigrette (page 263)
salt and freshly ground black pepper

To serve
1 quantity sautéed potatoes (page 154)

Heat the butter and olive oil in a heavy-based frying pan over a fairly high heat until bubbling. Season the steaks and add to the pan. Cook for 4–6 minutes, turning halfway through, depending on whether you prefer your steak rare or medium. Transfer to a plate and set aside to rest for a few minutes.

Drain the excess oil from the pan and add the tomatoes, olives and berries. Cook lightly, stirring, for 1 minute, then add to the vinaigrette.

Cut the steaks on the diagonal into equal pieces and serve with the vinaigrette drizzled over the top. Serve with the sautéed potatoes.

Osso buco

I like to encourage people to eat this stewed shin of veal with their fingers – so much easier than fiddling around with a knife and fork! When osso buco is done well, it's heaven for carnivores. Ask your butcher to cut up the veal shin for you, and make sure all the vegetables are cut into pieces of roughly the same size so that they cook evenly.

Serves 4

100 ml olive oil
handful of plain flour, for dusting
1 veal shin, cut into pieces 5 cm thick
1 onion, roughly chopped
1 carrot, roughly chopped
1 leek, roughly chopped
1 celery stick, roughly chopped
1 head of garlic, cut horizontally through the middle
4 sprigs of fresh thyme
2 bay leaves
5 white peppercorns, crushed
200 ml white wine
250 ml Chicken stock (page 260)
2 tomatoes, cut into quarters
salt and freshly ground black pepper

Heat the oil in a large pan or casserole over a high heat. Lightly flour the veal and add to the pan in a single layer. Cook for 2–3 minutes on each side until lightly coloured. Remove from the pan and set aside.

Add the onion, carrot, leek, celery and garlic to the pan and cook for 3–4 minutes, or until light golden in colour. Add the thyme, bay leaves, peppercorns and a little salt, and stir well. Arrange the pieces of veal on top of the vegetables in a single layer. Add the wine and boil until reduced by half. Add the stock and tomatoes and season well. Reduce the heat, cover with a cartouche (a circle of baking parchment) and a lid, and simmer for 2–3 hours, or until the meat is so tender that it falls off the bone easily.

Braised beef in red wine

For this incredibly rich, wintry dish, you need good-quality beef with a lot of natural fat running through it. It cooks slowly, like a French daube, and after three hours it will be so melting and tender that you should be able to cut through it with a spoon. Serve it with something that will soak up all those lovely juices; soft polenta (page 101) or mashed potato is ideal.

Serves 4

800 g diced beef brisket
2 tbsp vegetable oil
750 ml red wine (a Barolo is best, or a good Primitivo)
250 ml Chicken stock (see page 260)
3–4 tbsp olive oil
2 carrots, sliced
20 baby onions, peeled
salt and freshly ground black pepper
handful of fresh flatleaf parsley leaves, to serve

Season the beef. Heat the vegetable oil in a large, heavy-based pan over a high heat. When very hot, add the beef. Allow the meat to colour without stirring or moving it around in the pan – when it's coloured on one side, then turn it and colour on the other side. If you don't have a pan large enough to take all the meat in one go, cook it in batches. You mustn't overload the pan or the beef will stew and steam rather than caramelize.

When the meat is nicely brown on all sides, add the wine and bring to the boil. Reduce the heat and simmer until almost all the wine has evaporated: this should take about 10–12 minutes.

Add the stock and bring to the boil again. At this point, reduce the heat and cover with a lid. Simmer for 1½ hours.

Meanwhile, heat the olive oil in a pan over a medium heat. Add the carrots and onions and sauté until golden brown, about 5 minutes. Remove from the heat and set aside.

When the beef has been cooking for 1½ hours, add the cooked vegetables and stir together. Replace the lid and continue to simmer for 45 minutes to 1 hour. Add a little water if the beef looks at all dry.

After 2–3 hours the beef should be soft and falling apart. It can be taken to the table and served immediately, with the parsley leaves scattered over, or kept in the fridge overnight and eaten the next day, which will give all the delicious flavours a chance to meld and develop.

Vegetables and Salads

As you wander past people's gardens in Bardi, the delicious smells of fresh tomatoes and rosemary are intoxicating. My mother to this day grows her own bitter salad leaves in her garden in Essex. But in the UK and United States we seem to have lost touch with where our produce comes from. Recently my little nephews, Finn and Billy, were over from New York and while chatting to them I realised that, great eaters though they are, they have no real idea of where food comes from. My Uncle Ren decided to take them up to an allotment he shares in Dulwich, and the planned 'quick trip' in the car ended up being a three-hour visit. The kids absolutely adored it: carrots growing from the ground, raspberries on bushes – they were fascinated to see where food comes from, with not a cellophane wrapper in sight.

Salads can be as simple or as complicated as you like. For instance, the Broad bean, pancetta and courgette salad (page 169) is a posh restaurant version of a very simple, seasonal dish. The vital points to bear in mind with salads are how you serve them, when you serve them, and how they're dressed. You should never serve any salad ingredients straight from the fridge – always return them to room temperature first.

I like to vary my salads by adding extra ingredients, such as nuts and raisins. This is actually a southern Italian habit deriving from the Moorish influence on their cuisine. But a great and simple way to introduce a bit of variety is to make the most of the massive range of vinegars that is available these days. Try not to reach automatically for the balsamic. Sherry, cider and tarragon vinegars, for instance, can give a salad a completely different character. Of equal importance to the vinegar is the oil. Extra virgin olive oil is available everywhere these days, and I'm not going to insist you splash out on the expensive stuff if you find an everyday olive oil that suits your taste buds. But beware of leaving it in a hot place or buying huge quantities because it can go off quite quickly. I advocate getting a smallish bottle and using it up regularly. One of the best olive oils in the world, Manni, is available only in 100 ml bottles.

Finally, did I mention how versatile salads and vegetables are? You could serve any of the salads here as starters or as part of an antipasti selection. And plenty of the recipes in this chapter would make great vegetarian meals in their own right, such as Peperonata, Aubergine parmigiana and Mushroom ragù (pages 172, 178 and 182).

Artichoke salad

This seasonal salad is ideal for the summer months. The full-size globe artichokes are braised in stock to make them soft and tasty, while the baby ones are pickled to add a very refreshing contrast. You can serve the pickled baby artichokes on their own as an antipasto, if you don't want to make the whole salad (see photograph).

Serves 4
4 globe artichokes
3 tbsp olive oil
100 ml Chicken stock (page 260)
8 baby artichokes
½ frisée lettuce
1 quantity Classic vinaigrette (page 262)
2 tsp chopped fresh flatleaf parsley
salt and freshly ground black pepper

For the pickling liquor
125 ml olive oil
125 ml white wine vinegar
½ banana shallot, sliced
1 lemon, thinly sliced
1 bay leaf
1 sprig of fresh thyme
4 peppercorns
4 coriander seeds
pinch of rock salt

Place all the pickling liquor ingredients in a pan with 500 ml water and bring to the boil. Remove from the heat and set aside.

Cut the stalks off the globe artichokes. Pull off the outer leaves, then peel the side where the stalk was attached, removing all the knobbly bits and exposing the flesh. Cut off the remaining leaves and scrape off all the hairy bits (the 'choke'). You will be left with just the heart of the artichoke. Cut each heart into 6 pieces.

Heat the olive oil in a frying pan and add the pieces of artichoke. Season well and cook, turning, until golden. Reduce the heat and add the chicken stock a tablespoon at a time, waiting for each addition to be absorbed before adding the next. This should take about 10 minutes. Check that the artichokes are cooked by piercing with the point of a knife – the flesh should be soft. Remove from the heat and set aside at room temperature.

Prepare the baby artichokes in the same way as the globe artichokes, only leave them whole and don't cut off the stalks. Add to the pickling liquor and return to the heat. Bring to the boil, then reduce the heat and simmer for 10 minutes. Remove from the heat and leave the artichokes to cool in the liquor.

When cool, remove the baby artichokes from the liquor. Combine both types of artichoke with the frisée lettuce in a serving bowl. Dress with the vinaigrette and finish by scattering with the parsley. Serve at room temperature.

Raw mushroom salad

Emilia-Romagna is known for its wild mushrooms, and you could use pretty much any meaty variety in this dish (e.g. ceps, girolles, white Portobello). The cep season starts in September, and these wonderful mushrooms need no cooking whatsoever – simply slice them very thinly, sprinkle with a little olive oil and salt and the dish is made.

Serves 2
4 large fresh ceps, wiped clean with
a damp cloth
100 g rocket
½ small summer truffle, thinly sliced
1 quantity Classic vinaigrette (page 262)
salt and freshly ground black pepper
handful of Parmesan shavings, to serve

Using a sharp knife, slice the ceps as thinly as possible.

Put the ceps, rocket and truffle in a bowl and mix together, being very careful not to break up the mushrooms or bruise the rocket leaves.

Dress with the vinaigrette and season to taste. Scatter over the Parmesan before serving.

Opposite
Checking the quality
of the mushrooms at
the market in Bardi,
August 2005

Deep-fried courgette flowers

Courgette flowers are very trendy in London restaurants these days, but they are only in season over July and August. They're so easy to cook – just dip in batter and put straight into a deep-fat fryer a few at a time. Tempura flour makes the lightest batter, and is widely available in supermarkets.

Serves 4
vegetable oil, for deep-frying
100 g tempura flour
150 ml ice-cold sparkling mineral water
50 g 'oo' flour, for dusting
12–15 courgette flowers with stems,
cut in half lengthways
salt and freshly ground black pepper

Preheat a deep-fat fryer or a large pan of oil to 180°C.

Put the tempura flour in a bowl and sit it over another bowl filled with iced water. (This helps to keep the batter mix cold, and therefore as light as possible.) Slowly pour in the sparkling water and whisk lightly, ideally with chopsticks. The last thing you want to do here is overwork the batter – lumps are fine.

Put the 'oo' flour in a large dish and add some seasoning. Toss the courgette flowers briefly in the seasoned flour, then plunge them straight into the tempura batter. Fish them out and lower carefully into the hot oil. It's best to do this in small batches so as not to overload the pan and reduce the temperature of the oil. Fry until light golden in colour.

Using a slotted or wire spoon, carefully remove the flowers from the oil and drain on kitchen paper. Season with salt and serve immediately.

Broad bean, pancetta and courgette salad

Make this in July and August when broad beans appear. I recommend you buy a big chunk of pancetta and chop it up yourself – it stores in the fridge for weeks. When you brown the pancetta, don't discard the cooking fat – add it to the dressing to give an extra depth of flavour.

Serves 4
75 g pancetta, cut into pieces
about 1 x 2 cm
200 g podded broad beans
(about 1 kg unpodded)
8 baby or 4 medium courgettes
4 tbsp olive oil
1 quantity Classic vinaigrette (page 262)
salt and freshly ground black pepper
10 walnut halves, roughly chopped,
to serve

Heat a frying pan over a medium heat and add the pancetta. Cook, stirring frequently, until the pieces are golden brown. Transfer the pancetta and fat to a bowl and set aside.

Bring a pan of water to the boil, add the broad beans and boil for 2–3 minutes. Drain and plunge into iced water; leave to cool a little before removing the skins.

If using medium courgettes, cut them into four lengthways and slice into pieces about 5 mm thick. Cut baby courgettes into 4–5 pieces on the diagonal.

Heat the olive oil in the frying pan over a medium heat and add the courgettes. Cook, stirring, for 2–3 minutes, or until they are a light golden colour. Add a little seasoning (remember, the pancetta is already quite salty), then add the broad beans. Cook for about 30 seconds to warm through, then add the pancetta along with its cooking fat. Mix everything together well and check the seasoning one last time.

Remove from the heat and stir in the vinaigrette while still warm. Serve on individual plates, with the walnuts scattered over.

Fresh almond, green bean and peach salad

There's no getting away from it – you absolutely have to make this salad in the middle of summer. The combination of fresh, creamy-white almonds with peaches and green beans is stunning, all finished off with a touch of tangy cider vinaigrette. If you can't get hold of fresh almonds, use whole dried ones: blanch them briefly in boiling water before removing the skins.

Serves 4

150 g green beans, topped and tailed
4 peaches
75 g fresh almonds, husks removed, then briefly blanched in boiling water and peeled
6 fresh basil leaves
6 fresh mint leaves
1 quantity Cider vinaigrette (page 262)
salt and freshly ground black pepper

Bring a pan of salted water to the boil and cook the beans for 4 minutes. Drain and refresh in iced water straight away. Cut each bean into pieces about 2–3 cm long. Place in a large bowl.

Cut the peaches into 4 or 6 wedges, depending on their size. Add the peaches and almonds to the beans and season to taste.

Finely chop the basil and mint – do this at the last minute or they will go brown – and add to the salad. Mix in the cider vinaigrette, check the seasoning and, if necessary, sprinkle over a little salt before serving.

Nonna's potato salad

I can't bear the potato salads sold in supermarkets – disgusting stuff with often raw potato doused in sugary mayonnaise. When Nonna made potato salad, she would cook the potatoes, slice them up while they were still hot and then add the oil and vinegar so that the potatoes absorbed all the flavours. This is the only way to do it.

Serves 4–6
4–6 large waxy potatoes, scrubbed
but skins left on
300 ml olive oil
100 ml white wine vinegar
½ tsp Dijon mustard
1 garlic clove, lightly crushed with
the palm of your hand
1 shallot, finely chopped
1 tbsp chopped fresh flatleaf parsley
salt and freshly ground black pepper

Place the potatoes in a pan of salted water and bring to the boil. Reduce the heat and simmer for about 20 minutes, or until the potatoes are soft when pierced with the tip of a knife.

Meanwhile, mix the oil, vinegar and mustard in a large bowl, and add the garlic to infuse. Season to taste and set aside.

When the potatoes are cooked, drain and cut into bite-sized pieces. This must be done while they are still hot. Add the potatoes and shallot to the vinaigrette and mix well. Don't worry if the potatoes start to break down slightly. Remove the garlic and check the seasoning. Scatter over the parsley just before serving.

Peperonata

This brilliantly versatile dish can be made in advance and stored in the fridge, served cold or hot, on its own or as an accompaniment. The flavour intensifies overnight, so it will taste even better the next day or several days later (don't keep it for longer than about a week, though). The strong flavours of peperonata demand something quite meaty that can hold its own, so I like to serve it with roast lamb or monkfish (pages 150 and 120). It also makes a great topping for Crostini (page 229).

Serves 4–6 as a side dish
50 ml olive oil
1 small onion, sliced
3 red peppers, seeded and chopped into 2 cm pieces
3 yellow peppers, seeded and chopped into 2 cm pieces
1 x 400 g can plum tomatoes
2 tbsp chopped fresh flatleaf parsley (optional)
2 tbsp chopped fresh basil (optional)
salt and freshly ground black pepper

Heat the olive oil in a pan and add the onion. Cook until soft and translucent, but without colouring, about 3–4 minutes.

Add the peppers and continue to cook gently until softened, again avoiding any colouring.

Season to taste and add the tomatoes. Continue to cook over a low heat until the peppers are soft, about 1 hour to 1 hour 20 minutes. If the peppers look dry at any point, add a touch of water.

Remove the pan from the heat, stir in the parsley and basil, if using, and serve with crostini or grilled slices of ciabatta.

Chicory, golden raisin and green bean salad

Adding nuts and dried fruits to salads makes them more interesting, and here the sweetness of the sultanas sets off the bitter chicory. I like to plunge the beans briefly into cold water as soon as they're cooked because this retains their vibrant green colour. It's also a good idea to dress the beans while they're still warm so that they take on all the flavours of the dressing. This is one salad you have to serve straight away – it won't keep in the fridge – so eat it all in one go.

Serves 4
300 g green beans
4 small chicory heads
150 g golden raisins, soaked in warm water for 15 minutes
1 quantity Red wine vinaigrette (page 263)
1 tsp wholegrain mustard
handful of fresh flatleaf parsley leaves

Bring a pan of salted water to the boil. Add the beans and cook for 4 minutes. Drain and plunge immediately into iced water. Drain and set aside.

Cut each chicory head in half lengthways and separate the leaves. Toss in a bowl with the raisins and green beans.

In a separate bowl whisk the vinaigrette with the mustard.

Add just enough vinaigrette to coat the salad. Check the seasoning. Finish by scattering the parsley leaves over the top.

Tomato, mozzarella and basil salad

While this classic Italian salad appears on menus everywhere, very few places make it well – often because they use cheap, rubbery mozzarella and watery, chilled tomatoes. The quality of the tomatoes in the UK is often pretty poor, so at the Connaught we roast the tomatoes in order to concentrate the flavour.

Serves 4
8 ripe plum tomatoes
8 ripe cherry tomatoes, halved
leaves from 6 sprigs of thyme
2 tbsp olive oil, plus extra for drizzling
2 tbsp sugar
1 garlic clove, sliced
2 x 125 g balls of buffalo
mozzarella, sliced
1 bunch of fresh basil, ideally
with small leaves
salt and freshly ground black pepper

To prepare the plum tomatoes, make a little incision with a sharp knife in the top of each one. Bring a pan of salted water to the boil and blanch the tomatoes in it for 10 seconds. Drain and plunge immediately into a bowl of iced water – this will make the skins easier to remove. Peel and cut in half lengthways. Remove all the seeds with a teaspoon.

Preheat the oven to 120°C/Gas Mark ½.

Prepare a roasting tin just big enough to hold all of the tomatoes: drizzle 1 tablespoon of olive oil inside, then sprinkle in salt, pepper and half of the sugar. Place the tomatoes in the tin, cut side up, in one layer. Drizzle with the remaining 1 tablespoon of olive oil and sprinkle with salt, pepper and the remaining sugar. Scatter the thyme leaves and garlic slices over and around the tomatoes.

Bake in the preheated oven for 1–2 hours until the tomatoes begin to shrivel up. Halfway through the cooking time, turn the plum tomatoes over and remove the cherry tomatoes.

Mix the cooked tomatoes in a bowl with the mozzarella and basil, and check the seasoning. Serve on individual plates with a drizzle of olive oil.

Aubergine parmigiana

This classic Italian dish takes a fair amount of preparation, but it's ideal for making in advance because it benefits from being left to rest overnight so that the flavour develops. Key to its success are a rich tomato sauce and thick aubergine slices. It makes a great starter or veggie main course with a green salad, but I love to serve it as an accompaniment to lamb, chicken, sea bass or halibut.

Serves 4
200 ml olive oil
1 small onion, chopped
1 garlic clove, crushed
1 x 400 g can of plum tomatoes
2 large aubergines
2 x 125 g balls of buffalo
mozzarella, sliced
bunch of fresh basil leaves
100 g Parmesan, freshly grated
salt and freshly ground black pepper

Put 2 tablespoons of the olive oil into a medium saucepan over a low heat. When hot, add the onion and garlic and cook for 3–4 minutes, until soft and translucent but not coloured.

Add the tomatoes, break them up gently with a wooden spoon, and simmer for 25–30 minutes to create a thick sauce. Season to taste. Press the sauce through a sieve into a bowl and set to one side. Discard the pulp.

Cut the aubergines lengthways into 5 mm slices and sprinkle with a little salt. Leave for about 10 minutes to release their excess moisture. Pat dry with kitchen paper or a tea towel.

Heat the remaining olive oil in a large frying pan and shallow-fry the aubergine slices; they should be only lightly coloured.

Preheat the oven to 190°C/Gas Mark 5.

To assemble the dish, spoon a third of the tomato sauce into a shallow ovenproof dish (about 25 x 20 cm). Add a single layer of cooked aubergines, slightly overlapping the slices. Follow with a layer of sliced mozzarella, a handful of basil leaves and a sprinkling of Parmesan.

Repeat the process, finishing with a layer of aubergine. Sprinkle with the remaining Parmesan and cook in the oven for 25–30 minutes, until a lovely, bubbling crust has formed.

Tuna, celery and haricot bean salad

Any kind of pulse can be used in this recipe, but don't skimp on the quality. The tuna should also be very good – either Italian, Spanish or Portuguese (Ortiz is a good brand), preferably in a jar rather than a can, and always preserved in oil, which you should drain off. You'll immediately taste the difference from the bog-standard canned tuna.

Serves 4
200 g tuna in oil, drained
2 celery sticks, peeled and finely chopped
1 x 400 g can of haricot beans, drained
2 small red onions, finely sliced
1 quantity Red wine vinaigrette
(page 263)
1 tbsp finely chopped fresh parsley
salt and freshly ground black pepper

Mix the tuna, celery, haricot beans and onions together. Season well.

Stir in the vinaigrette, and add the parsley just before serving. Taste and adjust the seasoning as necessary.

Mushroom ragù

This is a very versatile vegetarian dish that freezes well. You could serve it with pasta or polenta, or as the filling for a Bomba di riso (page 100). Buy the whitest porcini you can find – the brown ones can sometimes be too strong-tasting.

Serves 3–4

2 tbsp olive oil
1 small onion, finely chopped
1 small carrot, finely chopped
1 celery stick, finely chopped
1 garlic clove, crushed
1 sprig of fresh thyme
1 sprig of fresh rosemary
100 g dried mushrooms (e.g. porcini), covered in hot water and soaked for 20 minutes
25 g butter
2 tsp tomato purée
50 ml white wine
salt and freshly ground black pepper

Heat the olive oil in a heavy-based pan over a medium heat. Add the onion, carrot, celery, garlic and herbs and cook for 4–5 minutes, until soft, but without colouring.

Drain the mushrooms, reserving the soaking water. If the mushrooms are large, gently break them up.

Add the butter and mushrooms to the pan, season well and cook for another 2–3 minutes. Add the tomato purée and cook for 2–3 minutes. Pour in the wine and allow to bubble and reduce completely. Strain the mushroom liquor and add it to the pan. Bring to the boil, then reduce the heat and simmer for 45–60 minutes, until the mixture has a thick, rich consistency. Remove the herb sprigs before serving.

Opposite
Two generations of cooks in action: Auntie Maria helping me at home in Bardi, August 2005

Desserts

Italians don't generally 'do' desserts. In fact, I would usually choose a plate of cheese over a pudding. But there's no doubt that plenty of people look forward to their puds, and I have always enjoyed making sweet treats. Even when I was away at college, I would make Victoria sponges, and impress dinner guests with Semifreddo (page 219), which is incredibly simple to make but looks as if you've slaved over it for hours.

We always had fabulous tarts and cakes as kids – Mum loved baking, although Nonna could make only crème caramel and zabaglione. But my dad's Irish mother made the most delicious apple tart I've ever tasted, and it became a real favourite of Nonna's, along with the all-time classic Lemon meringue tart (page 202). In that way my two grandmothers were bound by food as well as by marriage.

As a family, we are just as likely to go to the local shop to buy puds as make them from scratch. I think this is because Italian pastry shops are fabulous. In the hills of Bardi on a Sunday after church, people stroll down to the cake shops and buy a tray of delicacies to eat with afternoon tea – the local speciality, Crostata (page 194) or perhaps Almond cake (page 186). The shop windows are packed with trays of little cakes and biscuits filled with crème patissière, coffee-flavoured cream or zabaglione (my favourite): beautiful bite-sized pastries that you order and pay for by weight rather than individually. Then they're packed into boxes and tied up with ribbon. As a child, I'm not sure what I thought was more lovely – the cakes or the packaging!

There are a couple of cakes that every single Italian woman makes, and each has her own variation. Every time my aunts Ilda and Maria send me a recipe, they've added something to make it recognizably their own. My mum in particular trusts no one when it comes to recipes; when she sees an unfamiliar addition she always questions whether it will work. I may offend her (and many other relatives) by admitting that I prefer my cousin Rosanna's crostata over anyone else's. She very kindly gave me the recipe, and I've included it here.

What I hope to show you in this chapter is the simplicity of Italian desserts. I often think people build up the dessert course out of all proportion, making it more complicated than it needs to be. Just use wonderful, seasonal fruit whenever you can and keep it simple.

Almond cake

Every little area of Emilia-Romagna has its own take on this traditional recipe; for example, some add lemon, others Amaretto. It's incredibly simple to make, and not at all heavy because it's fat-free and contains whisked egg whites.

This particular recipe comes courtesy of my cousin Antonia and Auntie Rosina. If possible, buy whole almonds with their skins on and blitz them in a food processor. You can use ground almonds if you really can't find whole ones, but you get a much nicer texture and flavour if you grind them yourself.

Serves 10–12
butter, for greasing
100 g self-raising flour, plus extra for dusting
300 g whole almonds, skins on
10 eggs, separated
300 g caster sugar
zest of 1 lemon
½ tsp baking powder
double cream, whipped, to serve (optional)

Preheat the oven to 160°C/Gas Mark 3. Line the base and sides of a 30 cm springform cake tin with baking parchment.

Grind the almonds in a food processor. Set aside.

Using an electric mixer, beat the egg whites in a clean bowl until very stiff.

In a separate bowl beat together the egg yolks and sugar until thick and pale. Gently fold the egg whites into the yolk mixture using a large metal spoon. Fold in the lemon zest and almonds. Sift the flour and baking powder together and then fold into the egg mixture.

Pour the mixture into the prepared tin and bake in the oven for 1–1½ hours. The cake is cooked when a skewer inserted in the centre comes out clean. Cool in the tin on a wire rack, then remove and serve with whipped cream, if liked.

Walnut cake

Like the Almond cake on page 186, this is not very sweet, but it is slightly heavier, with a nutty texture. It stores well, and can be served slightly warm with crème fraîche or ice cream.

Serves 8–10
175 g softened butter
175 g caster sugar
3 eggs, lightly beaten
1 vanilla pod, split lengthways and seeds scraped out
225 g self-raising flour
½ tsp baking powder
pinch of salt
75 g ground walnuts
icing sugar, for dusting

Preheat the oven to 160°C/Gas Mark 3. Line the base of a 25 cm springform cake tin with baking parchment.

Before you start, make sure all your ingredients are at room temperature.

Using an electric mixer, beat the butter and sugar together in a large bowl until light and fluffy. Gradually add the eggs, beating well after each addition. Add the vanilla seeds and beat thoroughly.

In a separate bowl, sift the flour, baking powder and salt together, then fold into the egg mixture with a large metal spoon. Finally, fold in the walnuts.

Pour into the prepared cake tin and bake in the oven for 1½ hours. The cake is cooked when the surface feels firm and springy to the touch. Cool in the tin on a wire rack. When cool enough to handle, remove from the tin and serve dusted with icing sugar.

Nicole's apple cake

This is the one recipe in the book from my sister-in-law Nicole. Clearly she can cook, but she doesn't really enjoy it! She made this amazing apple cake for Finn's birthday, and prompted the whole family to exclaim, 'Oh my God, Nicole can cook after all!'

Serves 6–8

200 ml apple juice
2 Cox's apples
225 g soft brown sugar
200 g softened butter, plus extra
for greasing
3 eggs, lightly beaten
200 g self-raising flour
crème fraîche, to serve
a little ground cinnamon, to serve

Preheat the oven to 180°C/Gas Mark 5. Butter a round 20 cm springform cake tin and line the base with baking parchment.

Place the apple juice in a saucepan and boil until reduced to about 50 ml. Remove and set aside.

Peel, core and roughly dice the apples, and place in a pan with the sugar. Cook over a medium heat for 15–20 minutes or until the apples have formed a purée. Remove and leave to cool.

Using an electric mixer, beat the butter and sugar together in a bowl until soft and light in colour. Add the eggs a little at a time, beating well after each addition. Fold in the flour and then finally fold in the apple purée and the reduced apple juice.

Pour the mixture into the prepared tin and bake for about 1 hour, or until a skewer inserted in the centre comes out clean.

Cool on a wire rack and serve with crème fraîche and a sprinkling of cinnamon.

Opposite
My nephew Billy
with his mum, my
sister-in-law Nicole,
eyeing up his own
birthday cake

Antonia's chocolate cake

My cousin Paul's wife, Antonia, is an excellent cook. Whenever I see her she has a new recipe. This gooey chocolate cake can be put together very quickly. We actually make a chocolate dessert at the Connaught that's very similar, but we give it a fancy name, such as 'fondant'. This version is much more homely, but the principle's the same. It is very important for all your ingredients to be at room temperature before you start; if they are chilled they could set the melted chocolate. So take everything out of the fridge well ahead of time.

Serves 8

100 g softened butter, plus extra
for greasing
flour, for dusting
200 g dark chocolate
(70 per cent cocoa solids)
200 g caster sugar
5 eggs, separated
2 tbsp self-raising flour
1 vanilla pod, slit lengthways and seeds
scraped out and reserved
250 ml liqueur, such as Cointreau,
Amaretto or brandy

Preheat the oven to 180°C/Gas Mark 4.

Lightly grease and flour a 20 cm springform cake tin. Line the base with baking parchment.

Break up the chocolate and place in a bowl over a pan of simmering water (taking care that the bottom of the bowl does not touch the water). Leave to melt. Remove from the heat, add the butter and mix until well combined.

Beat in the sugar, egg yolks, flour, vanilla seeds and liqueur, and mix together until smooth.

In a clean bowl, whisk the egg whites to form stiff peaks, then fold into the chocolate mixture.

Pour the mixture into the prepared tin and bake for 20–30 minutes or until a skewer inserted in the centre comes out clean. Remove from the oven and leave the cake to cool in the tin. When cold, remove from the tin and store in a cool, dry place.

Cantucci

I worked in Florence for six months after leaving Aubergine, and we used to make piles of these almond biscuits. We now make them at the Connaught and give them away as Christmas gifts. You can serve them with coffee or for dipping into a sweet wine, such as Vin Santo.

Makes 48
180 g softened butter
275 g caster sugar
4 eggs, lightly beaten
10 g baking powder
½ tsp salt
500 g 'oo' flour
½ tsp ground aniseed
175 g whole almonds, skin on

Preheat the oven to 150°C/Gas Mark 2. Line two baking sheets with baking parchment.

Using an electric mixer, cream together the butter and sugar until fluffy and pale. Gradually add the eggs, beating well after each addition.

Fold in all the remaining ingredients except the almonds and mix well. Stir in the almonds at the end.

Spoon the mixture into a piping bag fitted with a large plain nozzle. Pipe out 5 cm wide logs on the baking sheets, leaving a gap of 3 cm between each one. Bake in the oven for 25–30 minutes, until slightly risen and golden brown.

Transfer to a wire rack and leave until just cool enough to handle (they still need to be warm so that you can slice them). Reduce the oven temperature to 120°C/Gas Mark ½.

Cut the cantucci diagonally into 1 cm slices, spread them out on the baking sheets and return to the oven for a further 20 minutes, turning halfway through cooking. Remove and cool completely before serving. These biscuits can be stored in an airtight container for up to two weeks.

Crostata

Go to any family gathering in Emilia-Romagna, or even just drop in for afternoon tea, and you will be served a crostata (jam tart) of some description. Like most Italian recipes, this one was devised to make the best use of local ingredients – in this case, the amazing plums that grow in the area. It's traditionally made with sweet pastry and a very rich, thick, unsweetened jam that's made in the Bardi region. You won't be able to get hold of that without a special trip to Italy, but crostata is still great made with a naturally sweetened plum jam, or an organic jam with no added sugar (Hero is a good brand). You can vary the filling by using prune, apricot, strawberry or raspberry jam. Serve the crostata either hot or cold, and if you don't want to eat it all immediately, it keeps well in an airtight container for 2–3 days.

Serves 10–12
1 quantity Sweet pastry (page 247),
with the zest of 1 lemon added to the
sugar and flour
250 g unsweetened plum jam
icing sugar, for dusting

Preheat the oven to 180°C/Gas Mark 4.

Lightly flour your work surface and roll out two-thirds of the sweet pastry. Use it to line a 25-cm loose-bottomed flan tin. Fill the pastry base with the jam.

Roll out the remaining pastry to a thickness of about 2 mm. Cut out strips about 1 cm wide and use them to make a lattice pattern over the top of the jam.

Bake in the oven for 25–35 minutes, or until the pastry is golden brown. Cool on a wire rack and dust with icing sugar before serving.

Tiramisu

I'm willing to bet that anybody who dined out in the UK in the 1980s will have had a bad tiramisu experience. At that time it was really trendy and appeared on the menu of every trattoria in the country. It was invariably served up in a big slab with heavy sponge and too much booze. But made properly, it's very good indeed. Auntie Maria gave me this recipe: the secret is to make sure that the coffee is strong and the liqueur cuts through the sweetness. We make our own version at the Connaught in little cups, and serve it with biscuits.

Serves 6–8
4 eggs, separated
75 g caster sugar
100 g mascarpone
1 vanilla pod, split lengthways and seeds scraped out
200 ml espresso coffee
25–50 ml brandy (depending how boozy you like it)
12 sponge fingers
cocoa powder, to dust

Using an electric mixer, cream the egg yolks and sugar together until pale and fluffy. Add the mascarpone and vanilla seeds and whisk together to combine.

In a separate bowl, whisk the egg whites until they form stiff peaks, then fold them into the mascarpone mixture.

Mix the coffee and brandy in a shallow dish. Dip the sponge fingers into the liquid and use them to line the base of a serving dish or individual glasses.

Spoon the mascarpone mixture over the sponge, then dust the top with cocoa powder to finish.

Refrigerate for at least 8 hours (ideally overnight) to chill thoroughly before serving. This allows the flavours to develop.

Zabaglione

This is a dish that Nonna always made at Christmas and Easter. She would never weigh out the ingredients, always insisting on measuring by eye ('ad occhio'): one egg yolk plus one eggshell of sugar and one of alcohol. She'd empty the drinks cabinet in the process! Now my Auntie Viv makes the most amazing zabaglione. You can use any alcohol – Marsala is traditional, but sweet white wine can be used instead. The most important thing is that you don't want the flavour of cooked eggs, so whisk over a very gentle heat. Serve it with more amaretti biscuits on the side if you like. And finally, don't eat zabaglione and drive – it's very potent!

Serves 6–8

12 amaretti biscuits
10 egg yolks
250 g caster sugar
200 ml sweet dessert wine
(see introduction, above)
50 ml whisky
50 ml brandy

Put the amaretti in a bowl and crush with the end of a rolling pin. Take 6–8 serving glasses and line the bottoms with the crushed biscuits. Set aside.

Bring a pan of water to the boil – it should be big enough to sit a large bowl on top without the base of it touching the water. Place the egg yolks and sugar in a large bowl and whisk together with an electric mixer until pale and thick. Add the wine, whisky and brandy and whisk again.

Place the bowl over the pan of boiling water and whisk. The eggs will gradually become very thick and creamy – about 5–8 minutes. Once the whisk leaves an indentation in the surface of the mixture, it is ready.

Pour the mixture into the glasses and leave to set in the fridge overnight.

Lemon posset

In this classic English pudding the acidity of the lemon sours and effectively sets the cream. At the Connaught we serve a posh version with lemon jelly in a glass, but it's delicious simply with a light citrus fruit salad.

Serves 6
500 ml double cream
125 g caster sugar
juice of 3 lemons and grated zest of 1

For the citrus fruit salad
1 orange
1 pink grapefruit
1 tsp runny honey
zest of 1 lime, plus a squeeze of juice
if needed
1 tbsp finely chopped fresh basil leaves
(chopped at the last minute)

Put the cream, sugar and lemon zest in a medium pan over a low heat. Bring to a simmer without boiling, and cook for 3 minutes.

Add the lemon juice and bring to the boil. Reduce the heat and simmer for another 7–8 minutes. Allow the mixture to cool down slightly before pouring into individual glasses. Leave to set in the fridge overnight.

To make the fruit salad, slice off all the peel from the orange, then segment it by cutting the flesh away from between the membranes with a sharp knife. Do this over a bowl to catch all the juice. Repeat with the grapefruit. Cut the segments in half and combine with the juice, honey and lime zest. Taste and add a little lime juice if you feel it needs a bit of extra sharpness. Stir in the basil and serve the salad with the set lemon posset.

Apricot tart

You'll nearly always find a fruit tart on restaurant menus in Italy. The squidgy frangipane base makes this one soft, moist and delicious.

Serves 8–10
200 g softened butter
200 g caster sugar
4 eggs, lightly beaten
100 g plain flour
200 g ground almonds
½ quantity Sweet pastry (page 247)
10 ripe apricots, halved and pitted

Put the butter and sugar in a bowl and cream together using an electric mixer. Add the eggs a little at a time, beating well after each addition. If the mixture begins to curdle, sprinkle in a little of the flour.

Sift the almonds and flour, then fold into the butter mixture. Refrigerate until ready to use. This is your frangipane mixture. You will need to take it out of the fridge half an hour beforehand so that it is soft and spreadable.

Preheat the oven to 180°C/Gas Mark 4.

Roll out the pastry to a thickness of 3 mm and use it to line a 30 cm flan tin. Line the pastry case with baking parchment and fill it with baking beans, rice or dried pasta. Bake in the oven for 15 minutes. Remove the beans and paper and return to the oven for another 5 minutes. Remove from the oven and set aside to cool.

Spread the frangipane over the base of the pastry case. Place the apricot halves on top, cut side down, keeping them as close to each other as you can so that the tart is nicely packed with fruit. Bake for 25–35 minutes, until the apricots have turned a lovely golden colour. Remove from the oven and serve warm, or leave to cool, then remove from the tin and eat cold.

Lemon meringue tart

This is my mother's classic recipe, which she learnt in an English cookery class. Nonna absolutely loved it, and when she died Mum stopped making it – perhaps because it evoked too many memories and feelings. But when my nephew Finn celebrated his first birthday over ten years later, Mum brought along a lemon meringue tart – the first she'd made since Nonna died. That tart gave Mum closure and Finn his first taste of this delicious dessert.

Serves 6–8
½ quantity Sweet pastry (page 247)

For the lemon base
50 g caster sugar
3 tbsp cornflour
275 ml cold water
grated zest and juice of 2 lemons
2 egg yolks
40 g cold butter, diced

For the meringue topping
2 egg whites
100 g caster sugar

Preheat the oven to 180°C/Gas Mark 4.

Roll out the pastry and use to line a 25 cm loose-bottomed flan tin. Place a sheet of baking parchment inside and fill with baking beans, rice or dried pasta. Bake for 15 minutes. Remove the beans and parchment and bake for a further 5 minutes. Remove from the oven and leave to cool while you prepare the filling. Reduce the oven temperature to 150°C/Gas Mark 2.

To make the lemon base, put the sugar and cornflour in a bowl and add enough of the water to make a smooth paste.

Put the remaining water in a medium pan with the lemon zest and juice and bring to the boil. Remove from the heat and add the cornflour mixture, stirring well. Return to the heat, bring to the boil again, then simmer for about 2 minutes, or until slightly thickened. Remove from the heat again and allow to cool slightly. Add the egg yolks one at a time, beating well after each addition. Finally, beat in the butter. The mixture should be thick and glossy.

Pour into the baked pastry case and set aside while you make the meringue topping.

Put the egg whites in a large bowl and beat with an electric mixer until they form stiff peaks. Add the sugar a tablespoon at a time, whisking after each addition. When glossy, spoon on top of the lemon mixture, using the back of a fork to form peaks.

Bake for about 20 minutes, or until the meringue is golden brown. It may looked cracked on top, but don't worry – that's all part of its charm.

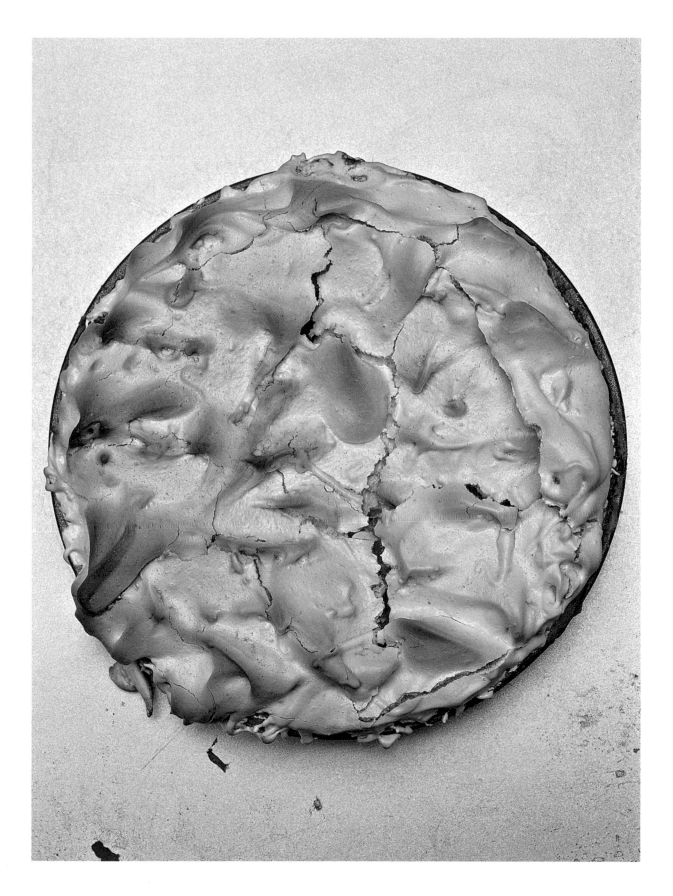

Pear and almond tart

Apologies to Italy, as this is a classic French dessert, but I just love the combination of pear, frangipane and crumbly pastry. It's a very moist tart because of the juice from the pears, so you don't really need to serve anything with it. But if you absolutely must have an accompaniment, you could eat it warm with vanilla ice cream melting over it, or a little pouring cream.

Serves 8–10
½ quantity Sweet pastry (page 247)
200 g softened butter
200 g caster sugar
4 eggs, beaten
100 g plain flour
200 g ground almonds

For the poached pears
250 ml Sugar syrup (page 248)
1 bay leaf
400 ml dry white wine
½ lemon, sliced
8 Comice or Williams pears, peeled and stalks left on

Preheat the oven to 180°C/Gas Mark 4.

Use the pastry to line a 30 cm loose-bottomed, fluted flan tin. Cover the pastry with greaseproof paper and fill with baking beans, rice or dried pasta. Bake in the oven for 15 minutes, then remove the beans and paper and bake for another 5 minutes. Remove from the oven and set aside to cool.

Put the butter and sugar in a large bowl and beat with an electric mixer until light and fluffy. Add the eggs a little at a time, beating well after each addition. If the mixture looks as though it might curdle, add a spoonful of the flour – this should bring it together again.

Sift together the flour and almonds, then fold into the egg mixture. This is your frangipane base. You can store this almond cream in the fridge until ready to use, but let it return to room temperature first so that it is easily spreadable.

Place the sugar syrup, bay leaf, wine and lemon slices in a pan just large enough to hold the pears and bring to the boil. Add the pears and cover with a cartouche (a circle of baking parchment). Place a small plate on top, so that the pears remain submerged, and reduce the heat. Simmer for 15–20 minutes, or until the pears are just soft enough for a small knife to pass through the flesh. Remove from the heat and leave the pears to cool in the liquor. Once cold, discard the stalks, cut the pears in half lengthways and remove the cores.

Fill the baked pastry case with the almond cream. Top with the pears, cut-side down, placing them as close to each other as possible.

Bake for 25–35 minutes, until the pears are a lovely golden colour. Remove and allow to cool a little before removing from the tin. Serve warm or cold.

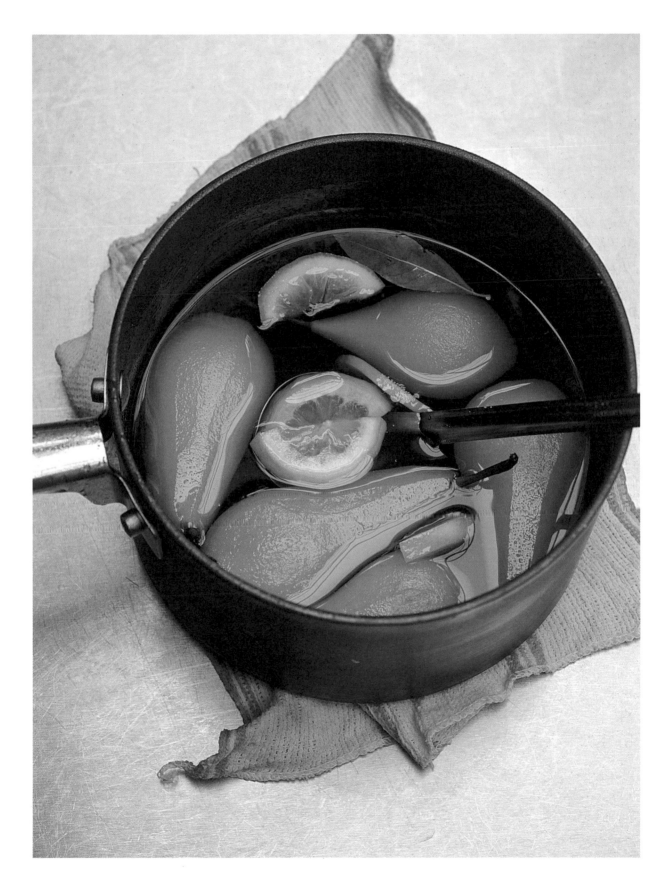

Figs in red wine

We put this dish on the menu when we first opened the restaurant at the Connaught. The idea was to serve figs, which were coming to the end of their season, with zabaglione to make them a little more sophisticated. My friend Camille came up with the idea of cooking the figs in red wine, then serving them hot with the zabaglione melting on top. We found we'd created something that you just want to eat and eat – it puts a stop to all conversation until you've scraped out the bottom of the dish. If you don't have time to make the zabaglione (page 198), just serve the figs with crème fraîche or a little double cream.

Serves 4
1 bottle good red wine, such as a Cabernet Sauvignon
500 ml ruby port
50 g sugar
12 ripe fresh figs

Place the wine and port in a pan with the sugar and bring to the boil. Allow to bubble until the liquid has reduced by half.

Meanwhile, peel the figs. Add them to the reduced wine mixture and simmer over a low heat until they are a deep red colour, about 10 minutes. When they are soft but not mushy – test by piercing with the tip of a knife – remove from the pan and place three figs in each serving dish. Return the poaching liquor to the heat and bring to the boil. Boil until it has reduced by two thirds and formed a thick glaze. Pour the glaze over the figs and serve with the topping of your choice.

Poached pears with Gorgonzola

This dish is illustrative of what you'd be served in a lot of Italian households after the main course – fruit and cheese – but I've made it slightly more sophisticated here. Always buy freshly cut Gorgonzola from a good cheese shop or delicatessen, never in a sweaty supermarket pack.

Serves 6

500 ml Sugar syrup (page 248)
750 ml good red wine, such as
a Cabernet Sauvignon
375 ml ruby port
1 cinnamon stick
1 clove
2 star anise
1 bay leaf
2 pieces of orange peel
6 ripe Comice or Williams pears,
peeled and stalks left on
200 g ripe Gorgonzola

Place the sugar syrup, wine, port, spices, bay leaf and orange peel in a medium pan and bring to the boil.

Add the pears to the poaching liquid. Cover with a cartouche (a circle of baking parchment) and place a small plate on top so that the pears remain submerged. Reduce the heat and simmer for 15–20 minutes, until the pears have just softened. Insert the tip of a sharp knife to test this – you don't want them to be too soft because they will continue cooking as they cool down in the poaching liquor.

Remove the pan from the heat and leave until completely cold. Lift out the pears and set aside. Return the liquor to the heat and bring to the boil. Continue boiling until it has reduced by two-thirds and formed a thick glaze.

Serve the pears drizzled with the reduced liquor and accompanied by a generous scoop of Gorgonzola.

Stuffed peaches

Another case of using the best seasonal produce and not messing around with it too much. You need really ripe peaches for this – don't even think about making it with unripe peaches, it will be disastrous! Preferably they should be on the turn, and baking them with a lovely almondy stuffing is a great way of using them up. This is a handy dinner-party dish, as you can cook it in advance and it will happily sit overnight in the fridge. You don't even have to heat it through, as it tastes great warm or cold – just make sure you get the peaches back to room temperature before serving with a little crème fraîche.

Serves 4
4 peaches
60 g amaretti biscuits
4–6 tbsp champagne or Amaretto liqueur (Disaronno)
butter, for greasing
crème fraîche, to serve (optional)

Preheat the oven to 220°C/Gas Mark 7.

Cut the peaches in half and remove the stone. Scoop out a little of the flesh with a teaspoon or melon baller, transfer to a chopping board and finely chop. Place in a bowl.

Crush the amaretti biscuits in a plastic bag with a rolling pin or in a food processor and add to the bowl of peach flesh. Mix in the champagne or liqueur to form a soft stuffing.

Fill the peaches with the stuffing and place in a buttered ovenproof dish that holds them quite snugly. Pour 50 ml water into the bottom of the dish to stop the fruit sticking and to make a syrup. Bake in the oven for 10–15 minutes, until the peaches are soft to the touch and the filling is crusty on top. If they look a little dry, add a touch more water.

Remove and serve immediately with any syrupy juices from the dish and some crème fraîche, if you like.

Grappa granita with melon

I made this summer dessert for my Uncle Renato, who never cooks. He hadn't tasted it before, but loved it and even said he wanted the recipe: the ultimate compliment. Grappa is a clear Italian spirit made from grape residue, basically what is left over after wine making. Its strong flavour melds well with the melon and mint to make a perfect, refreshing pud.

Serves 4–6
600 ml Sugar syrup (page 248)
200 ml grappa
1 cantaloupe or Galia melon, or 1 watermelon (or a combination)
4 fresh mint or basil leaves, finely sliced (optional)

Mix the sugar syrup in a jug with 700 ml water and the grappa. Pour into a shallow plastic container and freeze overnight.

Ensure the melon is at room temperature. Cut into bite-sized pieces and mix in a bowl with the mint or basil, if using.

Using a large metal spoon, scrape the granita into shavings. Place the melon in serving dishes and top with the granita. Serve immediately.

Crema catalana

Devised by Alistair, the pastry chef at the Connaught, this is an interpretation of the classic Spanish vanilla cream. We serve it with a sherry vinegar jelly and poached fruit (you can use poached pears instead of quince, page 208) so that it's like a sort of Spanish trifle.

Serves 4–6
500 ml single or whipping cream
100 ml milk
2 vanilla pods
2 egg yolks
80 g caster sugar

For the sherry vinegar jelly
2 gelatine leaves
375 ml good sherry vinegar

For the poached fruit
1 quantity Sugar syrup (page 248)
1 cinnamon stick
1 vanilla pod
1 clove
1 star anise
1 piece orange peel
3 quinces, peeled

To make the jelly, soak the gelatine in iced water until soft, about 5 minutes. Heat the sherry vinegar in a small pan and stir in the softened gelatine. When it has dissolved, pour the mixture into a square or rectangular plastic container and leave to set in the fridge overnight.

The next day, put the cream and milk in a medium pan. Slit open the vanilla pods and scrape the seeds into the cream. Add the vanilla pods themselves and bring the mixture to the boil.

Meanwhile, put the egg yolks and sugar in a bowl and beat with an electric mixer until pale and creamy.

Pour half the hot cream into the sugar mixture and beat well. Return this mixture to the pan containing the rest of the cream. Cook over a low heat, stirring constantly with a wooden spoon. The mixture should thicken enough to coat the back of the spoon – about 5 minutes. When you run your finger over the surface of the mixture in the pan, it should leave an indentation.

Remove from the heat and pour immediately into a bowl set over ice, still stirring constantly, to cool the custard quickly. If you don't have time to do this, simply cover with cling film to prevent a skin forming and leave to cool.

To make the poached fruit, put the sugar syrup in a pan with the spices and peel. Bring to the boil. Add the quinces and cover with a cartouche (a circle of baking parchment) and a plate to stop the fruit bobbing up. Reduce the heat and simmer for 10–15 minutes, until the fruit is soft but not overcooked. You should be able to pierce it easily with the tip of a knife.

Remove from the heat and allow the quinces to cool in the liquid. Store in the fridge, covered with cling film, until ready to use.

Cut the quince into even slices and place a few in the bases of individual glasses. Pour over the cooled cream mixture and leave to set overnight in the fridge.

Turn out the set jelly and cut into 1 cm squares. When ready to serve, top the crème catalan with 2 or 3 squares of the jelly.

Opposite
Focus on the food, boys.
My nephew Finn taking
nutritional advice from his
great-uncle Renato

Profiteroles with crème patissière

In Britain the word 'profiteroles' conjures up memories of the 1970s, when these rock-hard buns, stuffed with stale cream and smothered in gloopy chocolate sauce, were on every single restaurant menu. In Italy the soft choux balls have plain or coffee flavoured zabaglione piped inside, and you can buy tiny, bite-sized profiteroles in pastry shops.

Makes 15–20
1 quantity sweet Choux pastry
(page 246)
1 quantity Crème patissière (page 248)
vegetable oil, for greasing
icing sugar, for dusting

Preheat the oven to 200°C/Gas Mark 6.

Spoon the choux pastry mix into a piping bag. Pipe dessertspoon-sized amounts of the mixture on to a greased baking sheet, leaving a 3 cm gap between each mound. Bake in the oven for 10 minutes, then increase the heat to 220°C/Gas Mark 7 and cook for a further 15 minutes, until golden brown.

If, by the end of the cooking time, you feel the buns could be a little drier, pierce them with a sharp knife and return to the oven for a further 5 minutes. Transfer to a wire rack, pierce with a sharp knife if you haven't done so already, and leave to cool before filling.

Put the crème patissière into a piping bag with a nozzle 5 mm in diameter. Using the tip of a sharp knife, poke a hole in the bottom of each profiterole. Pipe the crème patissière inside until each one is full. Dust with icing sugar before serving.

Chocolate and vanilla semifreddo

This recipe (the Italian version of parfait) originally came from my Auntie Maria's mother-in-law, Ilda, and then Maria passed it on to Nonna, who passed it on to Mum, who passed it on to me – so it's a great example of Italian women passing recipes down the generations. It's a great make-ahead dessert that you can put in the freezer and forget. Be aware that it does contain uncooked eggs, and make sure you always use fresh organic ones.

Serves 6

100 g amaretti biscuits
splash of Amaretto liqueur (Disaronno)
100 g dark chocolate (70 per cent cocoa solids)
4 eggs, separated
100 g caster sugar
500 ml whipping cream, lightly whipped
1 vanilla pod, slit open and seeds scraped out

Carefully line the base and sides of a 1 litre plastic container with a large piece of cling film (you must ensure there are no splits or gaps in it). Set aside.

Crush the amaretti biscuits in a bowl and stir in a generous splash of the liqueur. Spoon the mixture evenly over the base of the lined container and place in the freezer.

Break up the chocolate and place in a bowl set over a pan of simmering water (taking care that the bottom of the bowl does not actually touch the water). Allow to melt. Once melted, remove from the heat and leave to cool a little.

Using an electric whisk, beat the egg yolks with the sugar until pale and thickened.

In a separate bowl, whisk the egg whites to form stiff peaks, then fold them into the yolks and sugar. Divide the mixture equally between 2 bowls. Add the melted chocolate to one bowl and mix well. To the other bowl add the cream, another touch of the liqueur and the vanilla seeds.

Remove the container from the freezer. Pour in the chocolate mixture first. Lightly tap the container on a work surface to level the mixture, then pour the vanilla mixture over the top. Tap gently again to even out. Cover with cling film and return to the freezer overnight to set (it needs to freeze for at least 12 hours).

When ready to serve, allow to soften slightly at room temperature, then tip on to a chilled plate and cut into slices with a knife warmed in hot water. Serve immediately.

Pannacotta with strawberries

Pannacotta has become one of those bastardized creations – go into a fancy restaurant and you're likely to find cauliflower or langoustine pannacotta! Essentially it's just cream, sugar and vanilla, set with a little gelatine. This is actually Gordon's recipe, and uses long-life cream to stabilize the mixture and ensure it won't be heavy or set too hard. Why reinvent the wheel when you've got this classic dessert and some delicious strawberries in season? Keep it simple.

Serves 8
3½ gelatine leaves
700 ml UHT cream
475 ml full-fat milk
140 g sugar
2 vanilla pods, slit in half
200 g strawberries, hulled, to serve

Put the gelatine leaves in a bowl. Cover with cold water and ice cubes.

Put the cream and 350 ml of the milk in a pan with the sugar. Scrape the vanilla seeds into the cream, then drop in the pods themselves. Bring just to the boil, stirring, until the sugar has dissolved. Remove from the heat and discard the vanilla pods.

Squeeze out the gelatine leaves and add to the hot milk mixture. Whisk well, then strain into a bowl through a fine sieve to remove any undissolved pieces of gelatine. Add the remaining 125 ml milk and allow to cool, set over another bowl of iced water. Whisk occasionally to prevent a skin forming.

When the mixture is semi-set, pour into individual ramekins or timbales and refrigerate overnight.

When ready to serve, lightly warm the dishes by dipping them in hot water before turning out on to individual plates. Serve with the strawberries.

Snacks

As a chef, I do many interviews discussing food, and one of the recurring questions is, 'What's your favourite food?' The easy answer (and the most natural one for a chef) is 'All food', but the real answer is 'Snacks'. I'm not talking about a packet of crisps: when I go home I like nothing more than a plate of cheese, salami, olives and salted almonds, all eaten with crusty bread.

The traditional snack in Emilia-Romagna is a torta made with various fillings, either spinach, potatoes or rice. It's absolutely delicious and a real family staple. My great-aunt Giovanna made the best Torta di patate (page 226), and passed on to me the trick of sprinkling polenta flour at the bottom of the torta and sugar on top, both of which combine to give it a lovely crunch.

I'm not denying that torta can be a lot of work, but it's worth it in the end. Nothing beats a beautiful potato cake fresh out of the oven, and the next day you can serve it cold. Once I went on a school trip to France and took cold torta as my packed lunch. Everyone else had sandwiches, crisps, chocolate bars and fizzy drinks. I gave a taste to one girl who turned her nose up at it, but my true friend, Laura, ate it and was full of compliments. Whether she was just trying to be nice, I don't know, but it pleased me at the time. Mum's larder never contained any processed foods; it was always stacked with fresh torta, olives and even leftover risotto made into deep-fried risotto balls (Arancini, page 228). Everything was tasty, fresh and healthy.

Although this book is dedicated to Italian cuisine and the dishes I grew up with, it would be a crime to ignore the influence and brilliance of Spanish cuisine. I adore chorizo, bacala fritters and deep-fried calamari, so I've put Spanish snacks on the menu at the Connaught and they've been a big hit. A few are also included here because I believe the principles of Spanish cooking are the same as in Italy – get the very best ingredients and do very little to them.

Torta di spinaci

I think spinach is my favourite variation on the classic torta recipe. My Auntie Viviana makes an amazing version of this, so moist and delicious that the whole family fights over the last piece. If we're having a family celebration, someone always makes a torta di spinaci – at Mum's seventieth birthday party all my aunts turned up with a torta of some description. Cheers, ladies!

Serves 8–10
400 g '00' flour
½ tsp salt
4 tbsp olive oil
100 ml ice-cold water

For the filling
1 kg spinach
4 tbsp olive oil
200 g Parmesan, freshly grated
2 eggs, beaten
¼ tsp freshly grated nutmeg
salt and freshly ground black pepper

Mix the flour and salt in a bowl, add the olive oil and water, and mix lightly until it comes together to form a smooth ball. Cover with cling film and leave to rest in the fridge for 1 hour.

Meanwhile, remove the stalks from the spinach, wash and dry the leaves, then chop them roughly. Mix with all the remaining filling ingredients in a bowl and season well.

Preheat the oven to 200°C/Gas Mark 6.

Remove the pastry from the fridge and roll out very thinly to about 30 cm square. Use it to line a 20 cm shallow pie dish. The pastry should be overlapping the edges so that it can be folded back over the filling.

Place the spinach mixture in the lined dish and fold over the surrounding pastry to cover it. Bake in the oven for 30–40 minutes, until the pastry is golden brown. Remove and serve either hot or cold.

Opposite
My lovely Auntie Viv,
queen of the torta di
spinaci, July 2006

Torta di patate

This version of potato cake is very local to Bardi; you have to roll the dough incredibly thinly so that it cooks through underneath. My great aunt Giovanna made a wonderful torta di patate: it was delicious straight out of the oven.

Serves 8–10
2 kg waxy potatoes
rock salt
2 tbsp olive oil
4 streaky bacon rashers, finely sliced
1 leek, finely sliced
40 g polenta flour
100 g Parmesan, freshly grated
2 eggs, beaten
4 tbsp caster sugar
salt and freshly ground black pepper

For the pastry
400 g '00' flour
½ tsp salt
4 tbsp olive oil
100 ml ice-cold water

Preheat the oven to 200°C/Gas Mark 6.

Prick the potatoes all over with a fork. Scatter a thick layer of rock salt into a baking tin, place the potatoes on top and bake in the oven for about 1 hour, or until soft. Remove from the oven and, when cool enough to handle but still hot, cut in half, scoop out the flesh and press it through a potato ricer (or through a sieve).

Meanwhile, make the pastry. Mix the flour and salt in a bowl. Add the olive oil and water, and mix lightly until it comes together to form a smooth ball. Cover with cling film and leave to rest in the fridge for 1 hour.

Heat the olive oil in a frying pan over a medium heat and add the bacon. Cook for 1 minute, then add the leek and cook for another 2 minutes until the leek is soft and the bacon golden brown. Remove from the heat and set aside.

Remove the pastry from the fridge and roll out very thinly to about 30 cm square. Sprinkle the polenta flour in the base of a 20 cm shallow pie dish, then line the dish with the pastry. The pastry should be overlapping the edges so that it can be folded back over the filling.

Put the leek, bacon, Parmesan and half the egg into the pastry case and season well. Cover with the potato, then fold the surrounding pastry over the top. Brush with the remaining beaten egg. Bake in the oven for 30–40 minutes, until golden brown. Five minutes before you remove the torta from the oven, sprinkle over the sugar and return it to the oven. Serve fresh from the oven or leave to cool.

Bacala fritters

*These little fritters are best made with cod you've salted yourself –
simply cover the fresh cod fillet in salt and leave in the fridge for at
least 24 hours – but if you don't want to do that, you can buy salt cod
at good fishmongers and delicatessens. Make sure the frying oil is
new and clean: if it's old or dirty, you can taste it straight away. The
mixture is bound together with choux pastry, which keeps the fritters
really light and fluffy.*

Serves 4

300 g salt cod
1 large Maris Piper potato
rock salt
500 ml milk
2 sprigs of fresh thyme
1 fresh bay leaf
2 garlic cloves, crushed
1 quantity savoury Choux pastry
(page 246)
squeeze of lemon juice
vegetable or corn oil, for deep-frying
salt and freshly ground black pepper

Place the salt cod in a bowl and cover with cold water.
Refrigerate for 24–48 hours, changing the water every 12 hours.
This will ensure that all the excess salt is removed and you're
just left with the lovely flavour of the fish. If you have made
your own salt cod, simply rinse it under cold running water
before using.

Preheat the oven to 200°C/Gas Mark 6.

Prick the potato all over with a fork. Scatter a thick layer of
rock salt on to a baking sheet, place the potato on top and bake
in the oven for about 1 hour, or until soft.

Meanwhile, remove the cod from the water and place in
a medium pan. Pour in the milk, then top up with enough
water to cover the cod completely. Add the thyme, bay leaf and
garlic. Bring to the boil, then reduce the heat and simmer for
10–15 minutes.

Remove the cod from the poaching liquor and, once cool
enough to handle, flake the fish into fairly small pieces. Place
in a bowl and discard the poaching liquor.

Remove the potato from the oven and, when cool enough to
handle, cut in half and scrape the flesh into the bowl of flaked
cod. It's important that the potato flesh is still warm when you
do this, otherwise the texture will be glutinous rather than
fluffy. Discard the potato skins. Add the choux pastry mixture,
lemon juice and some seasoning to the bowl. Mix well, then
shape into pieces the size of table-tennis balls. (At this point
you can freeze the uncooked bacala and then fry them from
frozen, though they will take slightly longer to cook through.)

Preheat a deep-fat fryer or a large pan of vegetable oil to
180°C. Fry the balls in batches until golden brown, about 3–4
minutes. Remove with a slotted or wire spoon and drain on
kitchen paper before serving immediately.

Arancini

This is a fantastic recipe for using up leftover risotto (pages 92–7). Filled with melting mozzarella, arancini (meaning 'little oranges') are perfect comfort food. If you like, roll them into smaller, bite-sized balls and serve them as canapés with drinks.

Makes 12–15 large balls,
20–25 smaller ones
½ quantity Basic risotto (page 92)
4 tbsp olive oil
250 g mixed wild mushrooms, wiped with a damp cloth and finely chopped
1 x 125 g buffalo mozzarella, finely diced
1 tsp finely chopped fresh flatleaf parsley
dash of truffle oil (optional)
200 g '00' flour
200 g fresh white breadcrumbs
3 eggs, beaten
vegetable oil, for deep-frying
salt and freshly ground black pepper

If making the risotto, spread it out on a flat tray to cool.

Heat the olive oil in a pan over a medium heat, add the mushrooms and cook for 3–4 minutes until golden brown. Transfer to a bowl, mix in the mozzarella and parsley, and season. If you have some truffle oil, you can add a dash of it to the mixture.

Add the risotto to the bowl and stir well. Take a heaped tablespoonful of the mixture and roll it between the palms of your hands to form a ball about 4–5 cm in diameter. Set aside on a plate while you roll the rest of the mixture.

Put the flour in a dish and mix in some seasoning. Put the breadcrumbs and eggs in two more separate dishes.

Take a rice ball and roll first in the flour, then in the egg and finally the breadcrumbs. Shake off any excess crumbs and set aside on a clean plate. Repeat with the remaining rice balls.

Preheat a deep-fat fryer or pan of oil to 180°C. Gently lower the arancini into the pan in batches and cook for 3–4 minutes, or until golden brown. Remove with a slotted or wire spoon and drain on kitchen paper. Serve immediately.

Caponata and crostini

Here's another recipe inspired by the cooking of southern Italy. Caponata is essentially an Italian version of the French ratatouille. Serve it as part of an antipasti selection, or as a starter by itself. The crostini (toasts) are made from stirato, the spindly Italian equivalent of a French stick, so use the latter if you can't find the Italian variety.

Serves 4

2 large aubergines, cut into 2 cm cubes
4 plum tomatoes
8 tbsp olive oil
1 large onion, chopped into 2 cm dice
2 celery sticks, sliced
1 red pepper, chopped into 2 cm dice
2 large courgettes, sliced into 1 cm pieces
50 g pine nuts, toasted in a dry pan until golden brown
50 g capers, rinsed
50 g green olives, pitted and roughly chopped
handful of fresh basil leaves, roughly chopped
salt and freshly ground black pepper

For the crostini

1 loaf stirato bread
100 ml olive oil, or enough to glaze the crostini lightly without saturating

Preheat the oven to 160°C/Gas Mark 3.

First make the crostini. Cut the stirato bread at an angle into 1 cm slices. Arrange on a baking sheet, drizzle with the olive oil and season. Bake in the oven for 5 minutes, or until the slices are golden brown. Remove and cool on a wire rack.

Put the aubergines in a colander and sprinkle with salt. Set aside for about 10–15 minutes to release their juices.

Meanwhile, prepare the tomatoes. Make a little incision with a sharp knife in the top of each one. Bring a pan of salted water to the boil and blanch the tomatoes in it for 10 seconds. Drain and transfer immediately to a bowl of iced water – this will make the skins easier to remove. Peel, quarter and de-seed the tomatoes, then cut each quarter into three.

Pat dry the aubergine with kitchen paper. Heat 6 tablespoons of the olive oil in a frying pan over a fairly high heat – it should be hot enough so that the aubergine sizzles but doesn't burn. If too cool, the aubergine will just soak up the oil. Fry the aubergine cubes in batches until golden brown, transferring the cooked pieces to a colander so that any excess oil drips out.

Wipe out the pan and heat the remaining 2 tablespoons of olive oil in it over a medium heat. Add the onion and celery and sauté for 3–4 minutes, or until golden brown. Add the red pepper and cook for 3 minutes, followed by the courgettes for a further 2–3 minutes. Now add the aubergine and tomato and cook for another 2–3 minutes, still stirring. All the vegetables should be tender and heated through, but not sludgy and soft.

Finally, stir in the pine nuts, capers and olives, season well and add the basil.

Spoon the mixture on to the crostini and serve. The caponata can be served warm or cold, and keeps well in the fridge for up to 2 days.

Chorizo and prawns

Spanish cuisine is currently enjoying great popularity outside Spain, and this recipe shows why. The combination of spicy chorizo and prawns might sound strange, but it works extremely well. They can be served as part of a tapas selection or as a nibble with drinks. If you like, you can thread them on to cocktail sticks to serve as a starter with salad.

Serves 4
50 ml olive oil
20 baby chorizos
200 ml red wine
24 raw prawns, peeled
1 tbsp chopped fresh flatleaf parsley
salt and freshly ground black pepper

Heat half the olive oil in a frying pan over a medium heat. Add the chorizos to the pan and cook, turning occasionally, until lightly coloured on all sides, about 8 minutes.

Add the wine, reduce the heat and simmer until the chorizos are cooked and the wine has completely evaporated. Remove from the heat and set aside until cool enough to handle. Slice each sausage in half lengthways.

In a separate frying pan, heat the remaining olive oil. Add the prawns and cook, turning halfway through, for 3–4 minutes, or until completely pink. Return the chorizo to the pan to heat through. Season and scatter with the parsley before serving.

Chorizo in red wine

As with the Chorizo and prawns (opposite), I recommend baby chorizos for this recipe, if you can find them. You can make this dish well in advance and store it in the fridge. Just heat it up when you want to eat, and serve with lots of crusty bread to dip into the unctuous red wine liquor.

Serves 4
1 tbsp olive oil
1 banana shallot or 2 ordinary shallots, finely sliced
20 whole baby chorizos, or
4 large chorizos
2 garlic cloves, crushed
250 ml red wine
handful of chopped fresh flatleaf parsley

Heat the oil in a frying pan over a medium heat, then sauté the shallot in it until soft. Remove from the pan and set aside.

Add the chorizo to the pan with the garlic and cook gently, turning occasionally, until lightly coloured on all sides.

Add the wine and cook until it has reduced to a thick sauce, about 8 minutes. Remove from the heat and allow to cool. When the chorizos are cool enough to handle, cut them into bite-sized pieces.

Return the chorizo pieces and cooked shallot to the pan and cook briefly to heat through. Scatter over the parsley before serving.

Manchego, olives and almonds

Manchego cheese is now readily available from most delicatessens and even some supermarkets. I like to dice it up and serve it with Spanish olives and salted almonds – a fantastic snack to serve with aperitifs before a meal.

Serves 6
200 g Manchego cheese
200 g mixed Spanish olives
200 g salted almonds

Dice up the cheese and combine in a bowl with the olives and almonds. Transfer to small dishes before serving.

Roasted nuts in rosemary and butter

I pinched this recipe from the Union Square Café in New York, where they serve these nuts at the bar. As soon as you walk in, you can smell the delicious herby aroma. Although cooked in butter, the nuts are not at all greasy – just lightly coated, sweet and aromatic.

Serves 4–6
500 g mixed nuts
250 g butter
pinch of cayenne pepper
pinch of paprika
½ bunch rosemary, chopped
50 g soft light brown sugar
salt

In a pan large enough to hold all the nuts in a single layer, melt the butter over a high heat until it starts to foam. Add the nuts and immediately reduce the heat to medium. Shake the pan constantly so that the nuts colour all over. Once they have browned, about 3 minutes, add the cayenne, paprika and rosemary, together with a little salt. Mix well and sprinkle in the brown sugar.

Remove from the heat, check the seasoning and drain through a colander. Allow to cool, then serve in bowls with a little more salt sprinkled on top.

233

Calamari

Every run-of-the-mill trattoria in Italy and the UK serves calamari (squid), but the result is very hit and miss. When done well, it's delicious. Done badly, and it's like chewing a bicycle tyre. Buy the smallest, sweetest squid you can, and add a touch of cayenne for a little kick.

Serves 3–4
50 g plain flour, seasoned with salt
and pepper
pinch of cayenne pepper
200 g cleaned squid (ask your fishmonger
to clean it for you)
vegetable or sunflower oil,
for deep-frying
1 lemon, cut into quarters

Put the seasoned flour in a large bowl and mix in the cayenne.

Cut the squid into 5 mm slices, but keep the tentacles whole. Toss the squid pieces in the flour until evenly coated, shaking off any excess.

Heat the oil in a deep-fat fryer or heavy-based pan to 180°C and fry the calamari for 2–3 minutes, until golden brown. Drain well on kitchen paper and serve immediately with the lemon quarters.

Deep-fried whitebait

This is a classic dish on both British and Mediterranean menus. It's unlikely that you'll find fresh whitebait readily available, but frozen ones are fine. Just defrost, toss them in flour, fry in oil and serve immediately. Don't leave them hanging around or they'll go soggy.

Serves 4
vegetable oil, for deep-frying
100 g plain flour
300 g whitebait
1 lemon, cut into quarters, to serve
salt and freshly ground black pepper

Preheat a deep-fat fryer or pan of oil to 180°C.

Put the flour in a dish and season well. Lightly toss the whitebait in the seasoned flour, shaking off any excess.

Lower the whitebait into the oil and fry for 2–3 minutes, or until light golden and crisp. Remove with a slotted spoon and drain on kitchen paper. Check the seasoning and serve with the lemon quarters.

Baby tomatoes stuffed with tuna

This recipe might sound as though it involves a lot of work, but it's really straightforward, and a great way of preserving any glut of tomatoes or red peppers you might have grown over the summer months. During the winter, you can just reach for a jar to serve with fish or cold meats, or simply with crusty bread – a little bit of summer in the refrigerator. They'll keep, sealed, for about three months.

Makes a 250-ml jar
20 baby tomatoes
100 ml red wine vinegar
150 g canned tuna, drained
½ bunch fresh flatleaf parsley, leaves chopped
juice of 1 large lemon
olive oil, to cover
salt and freshly ground black pepper

Make a small cut in the top of each tomato.

Put 800 ml cold water in a pan and bring to the boil. Add the wine vinegar, then add the tomatoes and cook for 30 seconds. Drain and plunge immediately into iced water. Peel the tomatoes and remove the stalks. Slice off the top of each tomato and scoop out the seeds with a teaspoon.

Put the tuna, parsley and lemon juice in a bowl, mix well and season to taste.

Carefully stuff the tomatoes with the tuna mixture, taking care not to get any on the outside. Place in a sterilized preserving jar, cover with olive oil and seal. Refrigerate until ready to use (bring back to room temperature before serving).

Variation
Stuffed baby peppers: Wash 12 baby peppers thoroughly, cut off the stalk ends and remove the seeds and membranes. Add to the boiling water and vinegar mixture and cook for 7 minutes. Drain and set aside to cool. Stuff with the tuna mixture, as above.

Baby peppers stuffed with goat's cheese

This is actually a Spanish tapas dish, which we serve at the Connaught as a snack with drinks. They make great party nibbles for vegetarians.

Serves 3–4
200 g sweet baby peppers
1 tbsp olive oil
150 g soft goat's cheese
1 pinch finely chopped fresh rosemary
½ tsp finely chopped fresh flatleaf parsley
½ tsp finely chopped fresh basil
salt and freshly ground black pepper

Preheat the oven to 200°C/Gas Mark 6.

Cut the peppers in half with a sharp knife, keeping the green stem attached. Remove the seeds and white core.

Place the peppers on a baking sheet and drizzle with the olive oil. Season and bake in the oven for about 5 minutes, or until soft. Remove from the oven and allow to cool.

Combine the goat's cheese and herbs in a bowl and check the seasoning. Spoon the filling into the pepper halves. (They can be prepared up to this stage in advance and set aside until needed.)

Return the peppers to the oven for 2–3 minutes to warm through the filling, then serve straight away.

Opposite
My brother Michael, at my East London party, July 2006

Fougasse

This classic French bread makes a lovely alternative to breadsticks or focaccia. Children especially enjoy making it, as the dough (even though it must be made with fresh yeast) is very easy and can be moulded into lots of fun shapes. As a tasty variation, you can make the slits a bit smaller and stuff them with cheese or tomatoes.

Makes 6

500 g strong bread flour, plus extra for dusting
10 g fresh yeast
2 tsp salt
300 ml warm water

Put the flour into a large bowl and lightly rub the yeast into it with your fingertips. Stir in the salt, then pour in the water and mix with one hand while holding the bowl with the other. Continue for 4–5 minutes, or until a dough starts to form, adding a little more warm water if necessary.

Tip the dough on to a clean work surface and knead for a good 10 minutes, or until it becomes smoother. Lightly flour the work surface and gradually form the dough into a ball, stretching it and tucking the edges under.

Flour the inside of a mixing bowl and put the ball of dough in it. Cover with a tea towel and let it rest in a warm place for about 1 hour, or until roughly doubled in size.

Once rested, preheat the oven to 230°C/Gas Mark 8. Place a baking stone or an upside-down baking sheet in the oven to get really hot.

Generously flour your work surface and transfer the dough without deflating it. Carefully stretch it out to a square measuring about 35 x 35 cm. Flour the top of the dough, then cut it into 6 equal rectangles.

Take 1 rectangle and use a sharp knife to make a diagonal slit across the centre, being careful not to cut right through the dough. Make 2 or 3 small diagonal cuts on each side of the central cut so that it resembles the veins on a leaf.

Using your fingers, open out the cuts, then work the fougasse so that the desired shape is obtained (see photograph opposite). Repeat the cutting and shaping process with the remaining rectangles.

Slide the fougasses on to the hot baking stone or sheet, spray some water into the bottom of the oven (this helps the bread to rise), then bake the bread for 10–12 minutes, or until golden brown. Remove and cool on a wire rack.

Focaccia

Like so many traditional Italian recipes, focaccia varies from region to region. The best I've tasted was in Liguria, where it's made with lots of olive oil. The crust should be salty and crisp, and when you're mixing the dough, don't be afraid of making it too wet. It can never be too wet – just trust me on this – it will come together. Too much flour and you end up with something resembling a doorstop.

Makes 1 large loaf
1 tsp fresh yeast
150 ml warm water
2 tsp salt
480 g strong white bread flour
150 ml cool water
1½ tbsp olive oil, plus extra for brushing
75 g Biga (see page 254)
3 sprigs fresh rosemary
1 tsp rock salt, for garnish

Dissolve the yeast in the warm water and leave to stand for about 15 minutes, until creamy.

Meanwhile, mix the salt and flour in a large mixing bowl. Form a well in the centre and add the yeast mixture, cool water, olive oil and biga. Stir together using a wooden spoon until the all the ingredients are combined. Turn it on to a floured work surface and knead until smooth and elastic – about 20 minutes. Shape the dough into a ball.

Grease a large bowl with olive oil, place the dough inside and turn it over so that it is fully coated in oil. Cover the bowl with a tea towel and leave to rest at room temperature for about 1½ hours, or until the dough has doubled in size.

After this time, punch the dough to deflate it. Fold the edges into the centre, then turn the dough over, cover again and leave to rise for a second time.

Turn the risen dough on to a flat baking tray and press into a square about 2 cm thick. Cover with a tea towel and leave to rise until doubled in size. If you want to add any topping to the focaccia, such as a few cherry tomatoes, place it on the dough before covering with the tea towel.

Preheat the oven to 180°C/Gas Mark 4 and place a baking stone or upside-down baking sheet inside.

Once the square of dough has doubled in size, brush it with olive oil and scatter the rosemary leaves on top. Sprinkle with the rock salt and slide on to the hot baking stone or sheet. Spray some water into the bottom of the oven and bake the focaccia for 5 minutes. Mist the oven again and continue baking until the bread is golden brown – about 30 minutes.

When cooked, place the focaccia on a wire rack and brush with more olive oil.

Basics

Italian ingredients are so readily available everywhere now that it's easy to
forget how difficult it was to get fresh Parmesan and olive oil in the UK during
the early 1970s. The only place in London where we could find authentic
Italian produce was Camisa & Son in Soho. My Uncle Renato was entrusted
with buying essentials whenever he was in central London, and when I was
old enough to go into London on my own at weekends I always had to check
with Nonna to see whether she needed anything from Camisa. If anyone was
travelling to Italy by car, Nonna would give them a shopping list a mile long!
And if we went to Italy ourselves, we would come back with food stuffed into
our cases. (I recall one occasion at the age of 12 when I struggled back with
salami, olive oil and wine crammed into my travelbag.) Ironically, this process
of shipping things back and forth now works the other way, and when we visit
Bardi we're always loaded up with English tea, biscuits and jelly.

Nonna was very organized – she had a cupboard in the garage where she stored all the basics that had been brought back from Italy. Salamis hung from the roof, there were countless tins of plum tomatoes and packs of the very best pasta, and there were copious supplies of the famous local plum jam. In a professional kitchen the larder is absolutely vital – indeed, it would be utter chaos if we had no basic store to draw on in case of emergency. I have to admit that at home I'm not quite as efficient – I tend to buy and use food on the same day purely because of the hours I work at the restaurant. However, if you do have time, I really recommend you to make and freeze or preserve the basic recipes in this section. The idea is that everything can be made in advance and stored for use at a later date.

With tomato sauce and stock in the freezer, and pasta and olive oil in the storecupboard, you'll never be stuck for a quick and easy meal.

Choux pastry

Many people are scared by the concept of choux pastry, but you shouldn't be. The secret is to beat it really, really hard – the mixture has to come away from the sides of the pan – and add the egg yolks when it's neither too hot nor too cold. If you're making this for a savoury dish, add a pinch of salt to the flour; for sweet dishes, such as profiteroles, add a teaspoon of sugar. You can freeze the pastry either raw or as cooked profiteroles.

Makes enough for 15–20 profiteroles
40 g cold butter, diced
50 g plain flour
1 tsp sugar or a pinch of salt (see introduction, above)
2 eggs, lightly beaten

Place the butter and 150 ml cold water in a pan and bring to the boil.

Meanwhile, sift the flour with the sugar or salt on to a large piece of baking parchment – this is so that you can slide it quickly and easily into the liquid.

When the water and butter come to the boil, remove from the heat and quickly add the flour. Beat together immediately with a wooden spoon until the mixture forms a ball and comes away from the sides of the pan.

Add the beaten eggs a little at a time, beating well after each addition. Use as specified in individual recipes.

Sweet pastry

This is the Italian version of sweet pastry, and can be made by hand or in an electric mixer using the paddle attachment. It's worth making a large quantity and freezing it in portions because it saves so much time and effort in the long run. Defrost it in the fridge and roll out while it's still cold – if it reaches room temperature, it's a killer to roll.

Makes enough for a tart serving 8–10
500 g plain flour, sifted
150 g caster sugar
250 g cold butter, diced
3 eggs, lightly beaten

Mix the flour and sugar together in a bowl. Add the butter and rub it in with your fingertips until the mixture resembles breadcrumbs. Pour in the beaten eggs and mix well, but don't overwork the mixture. Gently bring it together to form a dough. Cover and leave to rest in the fridge for at least 1 hour before using.

Crème patissière

The secret of making a good crème patissière, or sweet vanilla cream, is to sift the flour. This will ensure it's really smooth on the palate. The finished product shouldn't have any lumps or bits of skin in it.

Makes 500–700 g
35 g plain flour
40 g cornflour
50 g cold butter, diced
125 g caster sugar
750 ml milk
1 vanilla pod
5 egg yolks, beaten

Sift the flour and cornflour together into a bowl. Rub the butter into the flour with your fingertips until the mixture resembles breadcrumbs. Stir in the sugar and set aside.

Put the milk in a pan. Slit open the vanilla pod, scrape the seeds into the milk, then add the pod itself. Bring to the boil. When boiling, remove from the heat and take out the vanilla pod. Add the flour mixture to the milk and whisk vigorously. Return to the heat and cook over a medium heat for 3–4 minutes, whisking constantly. The mixture should become thick and glossy, with no lumps.

Remove from the heat and beat in the egg yolks. Pour the sauce into a roasting tin to cool it down quickly. Cover with cling film to prevent a skin forming. Once cooled, place in an airtight container and use as required. The crème patissière will keep for up to 48 hours in the fridge.

Sugar syrup

Makes 1 litre
500 g caster sugar
500 ml water

This can be used for sorbets, granitas and sweet sauces. It keeps for up to two weeks in the fridge.

Put the sugar and water in a pan and cook over a gentle heat, whisking constantly, until the sugar has completely dissolved. Raise the heat, bring to the boil and cook for about 5 minutes. Remove from the heat and leave to cool.

Opposite
Mum telling me that the risotto was overcooked, July 2006

Mustard fruits

Until I went to the three-star Del Pescatori restaurant in Mantova, Italy, I was under the impression that mustard fruits were difficult to make. They are, in fact, incredibly simple, but take three days to complete, and require mustard essence, which, I'm sorry to say, you can only buy in Italy. (Stock up when you're next over there.) It's impossible for me to exaggerate how wonderful these fruits are: I use them with meats (such as the roast duck on page 135), with cheese, with everything! They feature strongly in the cooking of the Mantua region around Cremona, but we also use a lot in Emilia-Romagna.

Makes 2 x 500-ml jars
1 kg small or baby pears, peeled but stalks left on
400 g caster sugar
10 drops mustard essence

Halve the pears, cutting through the stalk, then put them in a large bowl and mix with the sugar. Cover with cling film and leave at room temperature for 12 hours. This begins the fermentation process and brings out the juice of the fruit.

Remove the pears from the sugar, shaking off any excess. Place in a large dish. Put the sugar and pear juices in a pan, bring to the boil, stirring to dissolve the sugar, and cook for 5 minutes. Remove from the heat and pour the hot syrup over the pears. Cover and leave at room temperature for 12 hours.

Repeat the process of pouring off and boiling up the syrup three more times – so it will take 2 whole days from start to finish. The pears will release a lot of juice over this time.

The final time, measure out your remaining syrup. You'll need to reduce this to a third of its volume, so place it in a pan and bring to the boil. Boil until reduced by two thirds. Add the fruit to the pan, lower the heat and cook for 20 minutes. Leave the fruit to cool in the syrup. Once completely cold, transfer the pears to sterilized preserving jars. Add the mustard essence to the syrup, then pour into the jars and seal. They will keep, sealed, for up to 6 months.

Peach chutney

My cousin and her husband got married in the south of France, and after the wedding I couldn't resist gathering up the huge quantities of excess peaches that had fallen from the trees. I brought the peaches home and made a cupboardful of 'anniversary' chutney for my cousin. This quantity will make about eight jars, but it stores for months on end. If you like, you could substitute pears or apricots for the peaches.

Makes 3.5 kg
900 g demerara sugar
900 ml white wine vinegar
1 tsp cinnamon powder
6 pinches of saffron
1 tsp grated nutmeg
375 g onions, finely chopped
125 g root ginger, peeled and finely chopped
375 g sultanas
750 g tomatoes, skinned, seeded and chopped
20 peaches, stoned and cut into 2 cm chunks

Heat the sugar and wine vinegar in a large, heavy-based saucepan over a low heat until the sugar has dissolved. Stir in the cinnamon, saffron and nutmeg and continue to cook until the mixture has reduced to a syrupy consistency, about 3–4 minutes. Watch the mixture carefully as it can burn very easily.

Stir in the onions and ginger and cook until all the liquid has evaporated, about 40–50 minutes.

Finally, stir in the sultanas, tomatoes and peaches and continue to cook for 3 hours, stirring from time to time to prevent the chutney sticking and burning on the bottom of the pan. The mixture should have thickened considerably.

Remove from the heat and leave to cool. Spoon into sterilized jam jars or preserving jars and seal.

Biga

The biga is a basic starter dough that you can use as a base for any kind of bread (see the Focaccia recipe on page 242, for instance); you won't need the full amount given here but it keeps in the fridge for 4–5 days, so you can make fresh bread with it every day!

1 tsp dried yeast
90 ml warm water
400 g strong white bread flour
210 ml cool water

To make the biga, mix the yeast and warm water together and set aside until creamy – about 15 minutes.

Put the flour in a large bowl and make a well in the centre using a wooden spoon. Add the yeast mixture and cool water and stir together until well blended and stiff. Cover tightly and allow to ferment in the fridge for 24 hours before use.

Fresh tomato sauce

The only way to make this sauce is with the freshest and ripest of tomatoes. The best I've tasted was in Puglia, in southern Italy, because the tomatoes there are so flavoursome. If you can't find ripe tomatoes, don't even attempt this recipe – you're better off making a sauce with canned plum tomatoes (page 256).

8 tbsp olive oil
1 small onion, finely chopped
1 kg ripest tomatoes, cut into quarters
pinch of sugar, if necessary
salt and freshly ground black pepper

Heat the oil in a pan over a low heat. Add the onion and cook gently for 3 minutes, without colouring. Add the tomatoes and cook for 45–60 minutes, until the sauce has reduced and thickened.

Remove from the heat and pass through a sieve. Return the purée to the pan and cook over a low heat for another 15–20 minutes, until you are left with a lovely thick, jam-like sauce. Check the seasoning. If it still tastes slightly acidic, add the sugar. This freezes well or can be kept for up to 1 week in the refrigerator.

Basic tomato sauce

It's difficult to get really flavoursome tomatoes outside the Mediterranean, so don't be afraid to make sauces using canned plum tomatoes instead. My tip is to add a little sugar to cut through the acidity of the tomatoes – you'll be amazed at the difference it makes to the finished sauce.

Makes 4–6 portions
4 tbsp olive oil, plus extra for drizzling
1 onion, finely chopped
2 x 400 g cans plum tomatoes
1 garlic clove, finely chopped
2 tsp tomato purée
pinch of sugar
1 sprig of fresh rosemary

Heat the olive oil in a pan over a medium heat. Add the onion and cook for 5 minutes, or until soft and translucent.

Roughly squash the tomatoes with either your hands or a fork. Add them to the pan along with the garlic, tomato purée, sugar and rosemary. Lower the heat and simmer for 25–35 minutes, or until the sauce is thick and jam-like in consistency. Remove the rosemary sprig and finish with a drizzle of olive oil. Store in the fridge for up to 4 days, or freeze until ready to use.

Salsa verde

There are lots of variations on this green herb sauce, which is great served with fish or cold meats. It keeps well in a jar for a couple of weeks, or you can reduce the quantities if you want to make less.

Makes 125 ml
1 large bunch of fresh flatleaf parsley (leaves only)
6 tbsp baby capers, roughly chopped
6 tbsp cornichons, roughly chopped
12 anchovy fillets
3 garlic cloves, peeled
3 tsp red wine vinegar
olive oil

Place all the ingredients except the olive oil in a mini-food processor. Blend together, gradually adding enough oil to blend to a thick paste. Transfer to a bowl, cover with cling film and store in the fridge.

Opposite
My sister Anne, star of TV's *Can't Cook, Won't Cook* (see page 101), July 2006

Romesco sauce

This is a variation on the basic romesco crumb coating (see page 128) but mixed with some reduced stock it makes a lovely, versatile sauce that's great with fish and meat.

Makes 100 ml
50 g dried piquillo peppers
50 g stale white breadcrumbs
50 g almonds, lightly toasted in a dry pan
½ garlic clove
100 ml chicken or vegetable stock
(page 260–1)
salt and freshly ground black pepper

Place all the ingredients except the chicken stock in a mini-food processor and blitz until bright red in colour. Season to taste. Transfer to an airtight container and refrigerate or freeze until ready to use.

Place the stock in a pan and bring to the boil. Bubble until reduced to half its volume. Stir in 2 tablespoons of the romesco crumbs to make a sauce.

Fish stock

When you really get into cooking, you find it pretty unthinkable to throw anything away, particularly fish trimmings. These are wonderful boiled up and made into stock, and you don't have to simmer it for hours as you would a meat stock – in just 20 minutes you get the maximum flavour you're ever going to get from the bones. Turbot is one of the best fish to use for stock, as it's very gelatinous. You'll notice that only the stalks of the herbs are used: save the leaves for a salad or as a garnish for meat or fish dishes.

Makes 3 litres
2 tbsp olive oil
1 onion, roughly chopped
1 celery stick, roughly chopped
½ fennel bulb, roughly chopped
1 leek, roughly chopped
1 head of garlic, sliced in half horizontally
5 fennel seeds
3 white peppercorns
2 sprigs fresh thyme
1 bay leaf
500 ml white wine
2 kg fish bones, plus any available
fish trimmings
¼ bunch fresh chervil, stalks only
¼ bunch fresh flatleaf parsley,
stalks only
salt

Heat the oil in a large, heavy-based pan. Add all the chopped vegetables, the garlic, fennel seeds, peppercorns, thyme, bay leaf and some salt. Cook, stirring, for 5 minutes, or until soft and aromatic but not coloured.

Add the wine, turn up the heat and boil until the liquid has reduced by half. Add all the fish bones (not the trimmings) and enough cold water just to cover. Bring to the boil again, then reduce the heat and simmer for 20 minutes, regularly skimming off any scum.

Add the herb stalks and cook for another 10 minutes. Remove from the heat, add the fish trimmings and cover. Leave to infuse for 5 10 minutes. Pass through a muslin-lined sieve before using. This can be frozen or will keep in the refrigerator for 48 hours.

Chicken stock

If you buy chicken joints on the bone, use the wings and other trimmings for stock, as they provide a great deal of flavour. This stock can be refrigerated for up to three days, or frozen in individual portions for later use.

Makes about 2 litres
3.5 kg raw chicken bones
2 onions, roughly chopped
3 celery sticks, roughly chopped
2 leeks, roughly chopped
1 head of garlic, sliced horizontally through the middle
3 black peppercorns, slightly crushed in a pestle and mortar
salt

Put the chicken bones into a large pan and cover with water. Bring to the boil, then reduce the heat and simmer for 45 minutes, skimming off any fat and impurities as often as possible.

Add all the vegetables and the garlic and peppercorns to the pan and simmer for a further 1½–2 hours. Check the seasoning and add a little salt if necessary. Continue to taste and simmer until you feel that the flavour is right. Pass the liquid through a muslin-lined sieve before using.

Vegetable stock

To make a good vegetable stock you have to take it seriously; it's no good thinking you can just throw any old vegetable into the pot. You must spend time cutting onions, carrots, celery and leeks to the correct size, and don't bung in the trimmings. I remember on one occasion when I was working for Gordon that I didn't follow the recipe and ended up with a dodgy vegetable syrup. Gordon started screaming and the whole kitchen was in mayhem because vegetable stock is vital to so many dishes. I learnt my lesson that day.

Cut down the quantities if you don't want to make this much – however, it does freeze very well, so you can divide it up into smaller portions.

Makes 6 litres
5 leeks, cut into 2.5 cm cubes
20 carrots, peeled and cut into
2.5 cm cubes
10 onions, cut into 2.5 cm cubes
10 celery sticks, cut into 2.5 cm cubes
½ bunch of fresh tarragon, stalks only
½ bunch of fresh basil, stalks only
½ bunch of fresh chervil, stalks only
5 star anise
10 white peppercorns
10 fennel seeds
750 ml white wine
1 lemon, sliced

Put all the vegetables in a large pan and add just enough water to cover. Bring to the boil, reduce the heat and simmer for 8 minutes.

Add all the herb stalks, the star anise, peppercorns and fennel seeds and simmer for another 2 minutes.

Remove from the heat and add the wine and lemon slices. Allow to cool completely, then refrigerate for 24 hours to allow the flavours to infuse. Strain before use.

Classic vinaigrette

The classic French vinaigrette is based on white wine vinegar; get a good brand, as you can really taste the difference. This recipe can be adapted by adding a little garlic or Dijon mustard, whatever you fancy.

Makes 120 ml
20 ml white wine vinegar
100 ml olive oil
salt

Put the vinegar in a bowl, season well and mix until the salt is completely dissolved. Add the olive oil and whisk together.

Cider vinaigrette

Using cider vinegar makes a slightly different vinaigrette from the classic French dressing. The sweetness of the apples really comes through if you use a good organic cider vinegar.

Makes 125 ml
20 ml cider vinegar
2 tsp sherry vinegar
100 ml olive oil
salt

Put the vinegars in a bowl, season well and mix until the salt is completely dissolved. Add the olive oil and whisk together.

Red wine vinaigrette

I like to use a Cabernet Sauvignon vinegar in this dressing, as I love the flavour, particularly with meat. At the Connaught we use this vinaigrette as the base of a sauce to go with lamb – it makes a nice change from the usual gravy or thick fruity sauce, and is much lighter.

Makes 120 ml
20 ml good red wine vinegar
100 ml olive oil
salt

Put the vinegar in a bowl, season well and mix until the salt is completely dissolved. Add the olive oil and whisk together.

Following pages:
Family Tree

So many of the recipes in this book were inspired by or borrowed from members of my family that I really wanted to explain who they all are.

This family tree illustrates my Italian and Irish roots. My great-grandparents Bartolomeo and Giuliana owned Bosco, the family house in Bardi, Italy. All their children grew up in Bardi, including Clorinda, my Nonna, where she met my grandfather, Serafino Pesci. He emigrated with his brothers from Italy to South Wales (where Giuliana, my mum, was born), and from there to London.

My dad, Patrick Hartnett, was born in Cork in Ireland, and his family emigrated to Ilford, in Essex. It was here that my mum went to cookery school with his youngest sister, Margaret, and met my dad through her. The tree is still growing, with Finn and Billy, the next generation of Harnetts, and my cousin Laura's son, Jean. Hopefully they will grow to enjoy their food as much as us and pass on the family recipes.

Bartolomeo Margaritelli =

Maria
Joe = Pelopida
Johnny

Attilo
= Tina
Giuliana
Franco

Elisabetta
= Giovanni
Maria
Giovanna
Vittorino
Bertino
Gianino

Valentine Hartnett = Christina

Philomena
= William
Tina
Maria

John
= Angela
Clare
Deborah
Annabel
Felicity

Margaret
= Michael
Andrew
Joel

Clorinda
(Nonna)

Patrick Anthony = Giuliana Luisa Maria

Michael James Serafino
Nicole
— Finn Valentine
Billy

Angela Maria Clorinda

Anne Christin

Giuliana Antoniazzi

Gianni
=
Alda

Barbara
Giovanna
Anna

Manfredo
=
Irma

Giuliana
Maria
Massimo
Antony
Carlo

Rosina
=
Louis

Aldo
Paul

Aldo
=
Ilda

Rosanna
Linda
Angela
Giuliano

Dorino
Silvia

Gioachino Pesci
=
Giuliana

Charlie
Mario

Giovanni Pesci
=
Giovanna

Pino
Luisa

Serafino Pesci
=

Maria
=
Piero

Laura
=
Christophe

Jean

Viviana
=
Jonas

Patrik
Philip

Renato

265

Picture credits
All photographs by
Jonathan Lovekin except
for the following: pages 2,
8, 11, 12b, 24–5, 40, 77, 86,
98–9 and 147 © Angela
Hartnett; pages 12t, 164
and 183 © Jill Mead; and
page 15 © Paul Raeside.

Acknowledgements

Where do I begin? Well, in no particular order, just as it comes into my head ...

To the whole team at my publisher's, Ebury Press, with special thanks to my editor, Sarah Lavelle, who has shown unbelievable patience with the delivery of this book.

To Sam Wolfson for making the book beautiful, and Jonathan Lovekin, the best food photographer around. They are both true professionals in their own fields.

To Lisa Harrison, who tested all the recipes: if they don't work, blame her!

To Monika Aichele, for the family tree and calligraphy, Nigel Atkinson and team, and Summerill and Bishop for props used in the photographs.

To the whole Connaught team, who keep the place alive. Cooking really is a team effort, and without the guys at work – both back and front of house – I would not have been able to write this book. Special thanks to Neil, who runs the kitchen in my and Diego's absence, and to Chris, my F&B manager, who keeps everyone in order.

Thanks also to Neil Ferguson, who was my head chef at the Connaught for three years and has now gone to New York to run his own kitchen at The London. He was part of the team that helped me to gain my first Michelin star and has kept up those exemplary standards.

Finally on the Connaught team, a huge thank you to Diego, who is my right-hand guy – without him most of my working life would be a disaster.

To all my friends who have supported me with late-night eating and drinking to help me preserve my sanity. I can't mention everyone, but the Upminster girls and the Cambridge crew know who they are, as do Laura, Emer, Nicola, Larraine, Lara and Dan, Emma and John, and last but not least, David.

A few thanks to all the suppliers who contributed their produce for the photoshoot: Cove Shellfish, Patricia at La Fromagerie, Darren at Fairfax Meadow, Stefano Cavallini, Rudi at Brindisa and Danny at First Choice. In fact, thanks to all the suppliers who have supported me since I opened the restaurant doors. As I have repeated many times in this book, if the produce is good you need to do very little to it.

Continuing on the work front, to my fellow chefs Marcus, Mark, Jason, Stuart and Sarge – thanks for the continued support and mickey-taking.

A huge thanks to Gordon and Chris, my partners – they have shown great faith in me from the beginning and continue to do so.

Finally, thanks to my family on both my mother's and father's side – most of you have been mentioned in this book. Whether a Hartnett or a Pesci, we are all a product of our upbringing. I would have loved Nonna and Dad to have been alive to see this book; I am sure they know.

Two special thanks: to Ren, my uncle, who has read and re-read this book to check the accuracy of my family knowledge, and to Anne, my sister, who has to live with me and is sometimes treated as if she works for me.

Love you all and thank you.